Anonymous

Leaves of Grass Imprints

American and European Criticism

Anonymous

Leaves of Grass Imprints
American and European Criticism

ISBN/EAN: 9783744649254

Printed in Europe, USA, Canada, Australia, Japan

Cover: Foto ©ninafisch / pixelio.de

More available books at **www.hansebooks.com**

Leaves of Grass

IMPRINTS.

American and European Criticisms

ON

"LEAVES OF GRASS."

BOSTON:
THAYER AND ELDRIDGE.
1860.

July, 1855, Brooklyn, N. Y.—FIRST ISSUE of "Leaves of Grass," twelve Poems, 95 pages, small quarto.

July, 1855.—Note, as follows, from R. W. Emerson, promptly in response to sending one of the earliest copies of the issue:

CONCORD, Mass'tts, 21 July, 1855.

DEAR SIR,—I am not blind to the worth of the wonderful gift of "LEAVES OF GRASS." I find it the most extraordinary piece of wit and wisdom that America has yet contributed. I am very happy in reading it, as great power makes us happy. It meets the demand I am always making of what seemed the sterile and stingy nature, as if too much handiwork, or too much lymph in the temperament, were making our western wits fat and mean.

I give you joy of your free and brave thought. I have great joy in it. I find incomparable things said incomparably well, as they must be. I find the courage of treatment which so delights us, and which large perception only can inspire.

I greet you at the beginning of a great career, which yet must have had a long foreground somewhere, for such a start. I rubbed my eyes a little to see if this sunbeam were no illusion; but the solid sense of the book is a sober certainty. It has the best merits, namely, of fortifying and encouraging.

I did not know until I last night saw the book advertised in a newspaper that I could trust the name as real and available for a post-office. I wish to see my benefactor, and have felt much like striking my tasks and visiting New York to pay you my respects.   R. W. EMERSON.

WALT WHITMAN.

June, 1856, New York.—SECOND ISSUE of "Leaves of Grass," thirty-two Poems, 384 pages, 16mo.

May, 1860, Boston. — THIRD ISSUE, (inclusive of former Poems,) now just out in a finely printed 12mo. volume, 456 pages.

Leaves of Grass

IMPRINTS.

From the North American Review, (Jan. 1856.)

LEAVES OF GRASS. Brooklyn. 1855.

Everything about the external arrangement of this book was odd and out of the way. The author printed it himself, and it seems to have been left to the winds of heaven to publish it. So it happened that we had not discovered it before our last number, although we believe the sheets had then passed the press. It bears no publisher's name, and, if the reader goes to a bookstore for it, he may expect to be told at first, as we were, that there is no such book, and has not been. Nevertheless, there is such a book, and it is well worth going twice to the bookstore to buy it. Walt Whitman, an American — one of the roughs, — no sentimentalist, — no stander above men and women, or apart from them, — no more modest than immodest, — has tried to write down here, in a sort of prose poetry, a good deal of what he has seen, felt, and guessed at in a pilgrimage of some thirty-five years. He has a horror of conventional language of any kind. His theory of expression is, that, "to speak in literature with the perfect rectitude and *insouciance* of the movements of animals, is the flawless triumph of art." Now a great many men have said this before. But generally it is the introduction to something more artistic than ever, — more conventional and strained. Antony began by saying he was no orator, but none the less did an oration follow. In this book, however, the prophecy is fairly fulfilled in the accomplishment. "What I experience or portray shall go from my composition without a shred of my composition. You shall stand by my side and look in the mirror with me."

So truly accomplished is this promise, — which anywhere else would be a flourish of trumpets, — that this thin quarto deserves its name. That is to say, one reads and enjoys the freshness, simplicity, and reality of what he reads, just as the tired man, lying on the hill-side in summer, enjoys the leaves of grass around him, — enjoys the shadow, — enjoys the flecks of sunshine, — not for what they " suggest to him," but for what they are.

So completely does the author's remarkable power rest in his simplicity, that the preface to the book — which does not even have large letters at the beginning of the lines, as the rest has — is perhaps the very best thing in it. We find more to the point in the following analysis of the " genius of the United States," than we have found in many more pretentious studies of it:

"Other states indicate themselves in their deputies, but the genius of the United States is not best or most in its executives or legislatures, nor in its ambassadors or authors or colleges or churches or parlors, nor even in its newspapers or inventors — but always most in the common people. Their manners, speech, dress, friendships — the freshness and candor of their physiognomy, the picturesque looseness of their carriage, their deathless attachment to freedom, their aversion to everything indecorous or soft or mean, the practical acknowledgment of the citizens of one State by the citizens of all other States, the fierceness of their roused resentment, their curiosity and welcome of novelty, their self-esteem and wonderful sympathy, their susceptibility to a slight, the air they have of persons who never knew how it felt to stand in the presence of superiors, the fluency of their speech, their delight in music (the sure symptom of manly tenderness and native elegance of soul), their good temper and open-handedness, the terrible significance of their elections, the President's taking off his hat to them, not they to him, — these too are unrhymed poetry. It awaits the gigantic and generous treatment worthy of it." _

The book is divided into a dozen or more sections, and in each one of these some thread of connection may be traced, now with ease, now with difficulty, — each being a string of verses, which claim to be written without effort and with entire *abandon.* So the book is a collection of observations, speculations, memories, and prophecies, clad in the simplest, truest, and often the most nervous English, — in the midst of which the reader comes upon something as much out of place as a piece of rotten wood would be among leaves of grass in the meadow, if the meadow had no object but to furnish a child's couch. So slender is the connection, that we hardly injure the following scraps by extracting them.

"I am the teacher of Athletes ;
He that by me spreads a wider breast than my own, proves the width of my own ;
He most honors my style who learns under it to destroy the teacher.

> "The boy I love, the same becomes a man, not through derived power, but in
>   his own right,
> Wicked, rather than virtuous out of conformity or fear,
> Fond of his sweetheart, relishing well his steak,
> Unrequited love, or a slight, cutting him worse than a wound cuts,
> First-rate to ride, to fight, to hit the bull's eye, to sail a skiff, to sing a song, or
>   play on the banjo,
> Preferring scars, and faces pitted with small-pox, over all latherers and those
>   that keep out of the sun."

Here is the story of the gallant seaman who rescued the passengers on the San Francisco :

> "I understand the large heart of heroes,
> The courage of present times and all times ;
> How the skipper saw the crowded and rudderless wreck of the steamship, and
>   Death chasing it up and down the storm,
> How he knuckled tight, and gave not back one inch, and was faithful of days
>   and faithful of nights,
> And chalked in large letters on a board, 'Be of good cheer, we will not desert
>   you ;'
> How he saved the drifting company at last,
> How the lank, loose-gowned women looked when boated from the side of their
>   prepared graves,
> How the silent old-faced infants, and the lifted sick, and the sharp-lipped,
>   unshaved men ;
> All this I swallow, and it tastes good ; I like it well, and it becomes mine:
> I am the man, I suffered, I was there."

Claiming in this way a personal interest in everything that has ever happened in the world, and, by the wonderful sharpness and distinctness of his imagination, making the claim effective and reasonable, Mr. "Walt Whitman" leaves it a matter of doubt where he has been in this world, and where not. It is very clear, that with him, as with most other effective writers, a keen, absolute memory, which takes in and holds every detail of the past, — as they say the exaggerated power of the memory does when a man is drowning, — is a gift of his organization as remarkable as his vivid imagination. What he has seen once, he has seen forever. And thus there are in this curious book little thumb-nail sketches of life in the prairie, life in California, life at school, life in the nursery, — life, indeed, we know not where not, — which, as they are unfolded one after another, strike us as real, — so real that we wonder how they came on paper.

For the purpose of showing that he is above every conventionalism, Mr. Whitman puts into the book one or two lines which he would not address to a woman nor to a company of men. There is not anything, perhaps, which modern usage would stamp as more indelicate than are some passages in Homer. There is not a word in it meant to attract readers by its grossness, as there is in half the literature of the last century, which holds its place unchallenged on the tables of our drawing-rooms. For all that, it is a pity that a book where every thing else is natural should go out of the way to avoid the suspicion of being prudish.

From the Christian Examiner, (Boston, 1856.)

LEAVES OF GRASS. Brooklyn, N. Y. 1855. 4to. pp. 95.
LEAVES OF GRASS. Brooklyn, N. Y. 1856. 16mo. pp. 384.

So, then, these rank "Leaves" have sprouted afresh, and in still greater abundance. We hoped that they had dropped, and we should hear no more of them. But since they thrust themselves upon us again, with a pertinacity that is proverbial of noxious weeds, and since these thirty-two poems (!) threaten to become "several hundred, — perhaps a thousand," — we can no longer refrain from speaking of them as we think they deserve. For here is not a question of literary opinion principally, but of the very essence of religion and morality. The book might pass for merely hectoring and ludicrous, if it were not something a great deal more offensive. We are bound in conscience to call it impious and obscene. PUNCH made sarcastic allusion to it some time ago, as a specimen of American literature. We regard it as one of its worst disgraces. Whether or not the author really bears the name he assumes, — whether or not the strange figure opposite the title-page resembles him, or is even intended for his likeness — whether or not he is considered among his friends to be of a sane mind, — whether he is in earnest, or only playing off some disgusting burlesque, — we are hardly sure yet. We know only, that, in point of style, the book is an impertinence towards the English language; and in point of sentiment, an affront upon the recognized morality of respectable people. Both its language and thought seem to have just broken out of Bedlam. It sets off upon a sort of distracted philosophy, and openly deifies the bodily organs, senses, and appetites, in terms that admit of no double sense. To its pantheism and libidinousness it adds the most ridiculous swell of self-applause; for the author is "one of the roughs, a kosmos, disorderly, fleshy, sensual, divine inside and out. This head more than churches or bibles or creeds. The scent of these arm-pits an aroma finer than prayer. If I worship any particular thing, it shall be some of the spread of my body." He leaves "washes and razors for foofoos;" thinks the talk "about virtue and about vice" only "blurt," he being above and indifferent to both of them; and he himself, "speaking the password primeval, By God! will accept nothing which all cannot have the counterpart of on the same terms." These quotations are made with cautious delicacy. We pick our way as cleanly as we can between other passages which are more detestable.

A friend whispers as we write, that there is nevertheless a vein of benevolence running through all this vagabondism and riot. Yes; there is plenty of that philanthropy, which cares as little for social rights as for the laws of God. This Titan in his own esteem is perfectly willing that all the rest of the world should be as frantic as himself. In fact, he has no objection to any persons whatever, unless they wear good clothes, or keep themselves tidy. Perhaps it is not judicious to call any attention to such a prodigious impudence. Dante's guide through the infernal regions bade him, on one occasion, Look and pass on. It would be a still better direction sometimes, when in neighborhoods of defilement and death, to pass on without looking. Indeed, we should even now hardly be tempted to make the slightest allusion to this crazy outbreak of conceit and vulgarity, if a sister Review had not praised it, and even undertaken to set up a plea in apology for its indecencies. We must be allowed to say, that it is not good to confound the blots upon great compositions with the compositions that are nothing but a blot. It is not good to confound the occasional ebullitions of too loose a fancy or too wanton a wit, with a profession and "illustrated" doctrine of licentiousness. And furthermore, it is specially desirable to be able to discern the difference between the nudity of a statue and the gestures of a satyr; between the plain language of a simple state of society, and the lewd talk of the opposite state, which a worse than heathen lawlessness has corrupted; between the " εὐνῇ καὶ φιλότητι," or " φιλότητι καὶ εὐνῇ μιγῆναι," of the Iliad and Odyssey, and an ithyphallic audacity that insults what is most sacred and decent among men.

There is one feature connected with the second edition of this foul work to which we cannot feel that we do otherwise than right in making a marked reference, because it involves the grossest violation of literary comity and courtesy that ever passed under our notice. Mr. Emerson had written a letter of greeting to the author on the perusal of the first edition, the warmth and eulogium of which amaze us. But "Walt Whitman" has taken the most emphatic sentence of praise from this letter, and had it stamped in gold, signed "R. W. Emerson," upon the back of his *second* edition. This *second* edition contains some additional pieces, which in their loathsomeness exceed any of the contents of the first. Thus the honored name of Emerson, which has never before been associated with anything save refinement and delicacy in speech and writing, is made to indorse a work that teems with abominations.

From the United States Review, (New York, 1855.)

WALT WHITMAN AND HIS POEMS.

An American bard at last! One of the roughs, large, proud, affectionate, eating, drinking, and breeding, his costume manly and free, his face sunburnt and bearded, his postures strong and erect, his voice bringing hope and prophecy to the generous

races of young and old.   We shall cease shamming and be what
we really are.   We shall start an athletic and defiant literature.
We realize now how it is, and what was most lacking.   The
interior American republic shall also be declared free and
independent.

For all our intellectual people, followed by their books, poems,
novels, essays, editorials, lectures, tuitions and criticisms, dress
by London and Paris modes, receive what is received there, obey
the authorities, settle disputes by the old tests, keep out of rain
and sun, retreat to the shelter of houses and schools, trim their
hair, shave, touch not the earth barefoot, and enter not the sea
except in a complete bathing dress.   One sees unmistakably
genteel persons, travelled, college-learned, used to be served by
servants, conversing without heat or vulgarity, supported on
chairs, or walking through handsomely carpeted parlors, or
along shelves bearing well-bound volumes, and walls adorned
with curtained and collared portraits, and china things, and
nick-nacks.   But where in American literature is the first show
of America ?   Where are the gristle and beards, and broad
breasts, and space, and ruggedness, and nonchalance, that the
souls of the people love ?   Where is the tremendous outdoors
of these states ?   Where is the majesty of the federal mother,
seated with more than antique grace, calm, just, indulgent to
her brood of children, calling them around her, regarding the
little and the large, and the younger and the older, with perfect
impartiality ?   Where is the vehement growth of our cities?
Where is the spirit of the strong rich life of the American
mechanic, farmer, sailor, hunter, and miner ?   Where is the
huge composite of all other nations, cast in a fresher and
brawnier matrix, passing adolescence, and needed this day, live
and arrogant, to lead the marches of the world ?

Self-reliant, with haughty eyes, assuming to himself all the
attributes of his country, steps Walt Whitman into literature,
talking like a man unaware that there was ever hitherto such a
production as a book, or such a being as a writer.   Every move of
him has the free play of the muscle of one who never knew what
it was to feel that he stood in the presence of a superior.
Every word that falls from his mouth shows silent disdain and
defiance of the old theories and forms.   Every phrase announces
new laws; not once do his lips unclose except in conformity
with them.   With light and rapid touch he first indicates in
prose the principles of the foundation of a race of poets so
deeply to spring from the American people, and become in-
grained through them, that their Presidents shall not be the
common referees so much as that great race of poets shall.   He
proceeds himself to exemplify this new school, and set models
for their expression and range of subjects.   He makes audacious
and native use of his own body and soul.   He must recreate

poetry with the elements always at hand. He must imbue it with himself as he is, disorderly, fleshy, and sensual, a lover of things, yet a lover of men and women above the whole of the other objects of the universe. His work is to be achieved by unusual methods. Neither classic or romantic is he, nor a materialist any more than a spiritualist. Not a whisper comes out of him of the old stock talk and rhyme of poetry — not the first recognition of gods or goddesses, or Greece or Rome. No breath of Europe, or her monarchies or priestly conventions, or her notions of gentlemen and ladies, founded on the idea of caste, seems ever to have fanned his face or been inhaled into his lungs.

The movement of his verses is the sweeping movement of great currents of living people, with a general government and state and municipal governments, courts, commerce, manufactures, arsenals, steamships, railroads, telegraphs, cities with paved streets, and aqueducts, and police, and gas — myriads of travellers arriving and departing — newspapers, music, elections, and all the features and processes of the nineteenth century, in the wholesomest race and the only stable forms of politics at present upon the earth. Along his words spread the broad impartialities of the United States. No innovations must be permitted on the stern severities of our liberty and equality. Undecked also is this poet with sentimentalism, or jingle, or nice conceits, or flowery similes. He appears in his poems surrounded by women and children, and by young men, and by common objects and qualities. He gives to each just what belongs to it, neither more nor less. That person nearest him, that person he ushers hand in hand with himself. Duly take places in his flowing procession, and step to the sounds of the jubilant music, the essences of American things, and past and present events — the enormous diversity of temperature, and agriculture, and mines — the tribes of red aborigines — the weather-beaten vessels entering new ports, or making landings on rocky coasts — the first settlements north and south — the rapid stature and impatience of outside control — the sturdy defiance of '76, and the war and peace, and the leadership of Washington, and the formation of the constitution — the union always surrounded by blatherers and always calm and impregnable — the perpetual coming of immigrants — the wharf-hemmed cities and superior marine — the unsurveyed interior — the log-houses and clearings, and wild animals and hunters and trappers — the fisheries, and whaling, and gold-digging — the endless gestation of new States — the convening of Congress every December, the members coming up from all climates, and from the uttermost parts — the noble character of the free American workman and workwoman — the fierceness of the people when well roused — the ardor of their friendships — the

large amativeness — the equality of the female with the male —
the Yankee swap — the New York firemen and the target excur-
sion — the southern plantation life — the character of the north-
east and of the northwest and southwest — and the character of
America and the American people everywhere. For these the
old usages of poets afford Walt Whitman no means sufficiently
fit and free, and he rejects the old usages. The style of the
bard that is waited for, is to be transcendent and new. It is to
be indirect, and not direct or descriptive or epic. Its quality is
to go through these to much more. Let the age and wars (he
says) of other nations be chanted, and their eras and characters
be illustrated, and that finish the verse. Not so (he continues)
the great psalm of the republic. Here the theme is creative and
has vista. Here comes one among the well-beloved stone cut-
ters, and announces himself, and plans with decision and
science, and sees the solid and beautiful forms of the future
where there are now no solid forms.

The style of these poems, therefore, is simply their own style,
just born and red. Nature may have given the hint to the
author of the " Leaves of Grass," but there exists no book or
fragment of a book which can have given the hint to them. All
beauty, he says, comes from beautiful blood and a beautiful
brain. His rhythm and uniformity he will conceal in the roots
of his verses, not to be seen of themselves, but to break forth
loosely as lilacs on a bush, and take shapes compact, as the
shapes of melons, or chestnuts, or pears.

The poems of the " Leaves of Grass " are twelve in number.
Walt Whitman at first proceeds to put his own body and soul
into the new versification :

" I celebrate myself,
 And what I assume you shall assume,
 For every atom belonging to me, as good belongs to you."

He leaves houses and their shuttered rooms, for the open air.
He drops disguise and ceremony, and walks forth with the confidence and gayety of a child. For the old decorums of writing
he substitutes his own decorums. The first glance out of his
eyes electrifies him with love and delight. He will have the
earth receive and return his affection ; he will stay with it as the
bridegroom stays with the bride. The cool-breath'd ground, the
slumbering and liquid trees, the just-gone sunset, the vitreous
pour of the full moon, the tender and growing night, he salutes
and touches, and they touch him. The sea supports him, and
hurries him off with its powerful and crooked fingers. Dash me
with amorous wet ! then, he says ; I can repay you.

The rules of polite circles are dismissed with scorn. Your
stale modesties, he seems to say, are filthy to such a man as I.

" I believe in the flesh and the appetites,
 Seeing, hearing, and feeling, are miracles, and each part and tag of me is a
   miracle.

I do not press my finger across my mouth,
I keep as delicate around the bowels as around the head and heart,
Copulation is no more rank to me than death is."

No skulker or tea-drinking poet is Walt Whitman. He will bring poems to fill the days and nights — fit for men and women with the attributes of throbbing blood and flesh. The body, he teaches, is beautiful. Sex is also beautiful. Are you to be put down, he seems to ask, to that shallow level of literature and conversation that stops a man's recognizing the delicious pleasure of his sex, or a woman hers? Nature he proclaims inherently clean. Sex will not be put aside; it is a great ordination of the universe. He works the muscle of the male and the teeming fibre of the female throughout his writings, as wholesome realities, impure only by deliberate intention and effort. To men and women he says, You can have healthy and powerful breeds of children on no less terms than these of mine. Follow me, and there shall be taller and richer crops of humanity on the earth.

Especially in the "Leaves of Grass" are the facts of eternity and immortality largely treated. Happiness is no dream, and perfection is no dream. Amelioration is my lesson, he says with calm voice, and progress is my lesson and the lesson of all things. Then his persuasion becomes a taunt, and his love bitter and compulsory. With strong and steady call he addresses men. Come, he seems to say, from the midst of all that you have been your whole life surrounding yourself with. Leave all the preaching and teaching of others, and mind only these words of mine.

"Long enough have you dreamed contemptible dreams,
Now I wash the gum from your eyes,
You must habit yourself to the dazzle of the light and of every moment of your life.

Long have you timidly waded, holding a plank by the shore,
Now I will you to be a bold swimmer,
To jump off in the midst of the sea, and rise again and nod to me and shout, and laughingly dash with your hair.

I am the teacher of athletes,
He that by me spreads a wider breast than my own proves the width of my own,
He most honors my style who learns under it to destroy the teacher.

The boy I love, the same becomes a man not through derived power but in his own right,
Wicked, rather than virtuous out of conformity or fear,
Fond of his sweetheart, relishing well his steak,
Unrequited love or a slight cutting him worse than a wound cuts,
First rate to ride, to fight, to hit the bull's eye, to sail a skiff, to sing a song, or play on the banjo,
Preferring scars and faces pitted with small pox over all latherers and those that keep out of the sun.

I teach straying from me, yet who can stray from me?
I follow you whoever you are from the present hour:
My words itch at your ears till you understand them.

I do not say these things for a dollar, or to fill up the time while I wait for a boat;
It is you talking just as much as myself . . . . . I act as the tongue of you,
It was tied in your mouth . . . . . in mine it begins to be loosened.

I swear I will never mention love or death inside a house,
And I swear I never will translate myself at all, only to him or her who privately stays with me in the open air."

The eleven other poems have each distinct purposes, curiously veiled. Theirs is no writer to be gone through with in a day or a month. Rather it is his pleasure to elude you and provoke you for deliberate purposes of his own.

Doubtless in the scheme this man has built for himself, the writing of poems is but a proportionate part of the whole. It is plain that public and private performance, politics, love, friendship, behavior, the art of conversation, science, society, the American people, the reception of the great novelties of city and country, all have their equal call upon him, and receive equal attention. In politics he could enter with the freedom and reality he shows in poetry. His scope of life is the amplest of any yet in philosophy. He is the true spiritualist. He recognizes no annihilation, or death, or loss of identity. He is the largest lover and sympathizer that has appeared in literature. He loves the earth and sun and the animals. He does not separate the learned from the unlearned, the northerner from the southerner, the white from the black, or the native from the immigrant just landed at the wharf. Every one, he seems to say, appears excellent to me; every employment is adorned, and every male and female glorious.

" The press of my foot to the earth springs a hundred affections,
They scorn the best I can do to relate them.

I am enamoured of growing outdoors,
Of men that live among cattle, or taste of the ocean or woods,
Of the builders and steerers of ships, of the wielders of axes and mauls, of the drivers of horses,
I can eat and sleep with them week in and week out.

What is commonest, and cheapest, and nearest, and easiest, is me,
Me going in for my chances, spending for vast returns,
Adorning myself to bestow myself on the first that will take me,
Not asking the sky to come down to my goodwill,
Scattering it freely forever."

If health were not his distinguishing attribute, this poet would be the very harlot of persons. Right and left he flings his arms, drawing men and women with undeniable love to his close embrace, loving the clasp of their hands, the touch of their necks and breasts, and the sound of their voice. All else seems to burn up under his fierce affection for persons. Politics, religions, institutions, art, quickly fall aside before them. In the whole universe, he says, I see nothing more divine than human souls.

" When the psalm sings instead of the singer,
When the script preaches instead of the preacher,

> When the pulpit descends and goes, instead of the carver that carved the supporting desk,
> When the sacred vessels or the bits of the eucharist, or the lath and plast, procreate as effectually as the young silversmiths or bakers, or the masons in their overalls,
> When a university course convinces like a slumbering woman and child convince,
> When the minted gold in the vault smiles like the night-watchman's daughter,
> When warrantee deeds loafe in chairs opposite and are my friendly companions,
> I intend to reach them my hand and make as much of them as I make of men and women."

Who then is that insolent unknown ? Who is it, praising himself as if others were not fit to do it, and coming rough and unbidden among writers, to unsettle what was settled, and to revolutionize in fact our modern civilization ? Walt Whitman was born on Long Island, on the hills about thirty miles from the greatest American city, on the last day of May, 1819, and has grown up in Brooklyn and New York to be thirty-six years old, to enjoy perfect health, and to understand his country and its spirit.

Interrogations more than this, and that will not be put off unanswered, spring continually through the perusal of Leaves of Grass :

Must not the true American poet indeed absorb all others, and present a new and far more ample and vigorous type ?

Has not the time arrived for a school of live writing and tuition consistent with the principles of these poems ? consistent with the free spirit of this age, and with the American truths of politics ? consistent with geology, and astronomy, and phrenology, and human physiology ? consistent with the sublimity of immortality and the directness of common sense ?

If in this poem the United States have found their poetic voice and taken measure and form, is it any more than a beginning ? Walt Whitman himself disclaims singularity in his work, and announces the coming after him of great successions of poets, and that he but lifts his finger to give the signal.

Was he not needed ? Has not literature been bred in-and-in long enough ? Has it not become unbearably artificial ?

Shall a man of faith and practice in the simplicity of real things be called eccentric, while every disciple of the fictitious school writes without question ?

Shall it still be the amazement of the light and dark that freshness of expression is the rarest quality of all ?

You have come in good time, Walt Whitman ! In opinions, in manners, in costumes, in books, in the aims and occupancy of life, in associates, in poems, conformity to all unnatural and tainted customs passes without remark, while perfect naturalness, health, faith, self-reliance, and all primal expressions of the manliest love and friendship, subject one to the stare and controversy of the world.

From the Crayon, (N. Y. 1856.)

STUDIES AMONG THE LEAVES.

THE ASSEMBLY OF EXTREMES. — A subtle old proverb says, "extremes meet," and science, art, and even morality, sometimes testify to the truth of the proverb; and there are some curious problems involved in the demonstration of it. The loftiest attainment of the wisdom and worth of age only reaches to the simplicity and fervor of childhood, from which we all start, and returning to which we are blessed. Art makes the same voyage round its sphere, holding ever westward its way into new and unexplored regions, until it, doing what Columbus would have done, had his faith and self-denial been greater, reaches the east again. If the individual, Columbus, failed to accomplish the destiny, the class, Columbus, fails never. And so, in art, what no one does, the many accomplish, and finally, the cycle is filled.

We see this most forcibly in the comparison of two late poems, as unlike, at first thought, as two could be, and yet in which the most striking likenesses prevail, "MAUD," * and "LEAVES OF GRASS;" † the one as refined in its art as the most refined, delicate in its stucture, and consummate in its subtlety of expression; the other rude and rough, and heedless in its forms — *nonchalant* in everything but its essential ideas. The one comes from the last stage of cultivation of the Old World, and shows evidence of morbid, luxurious waste of power, and contempt of mental wealth, from inability longer to appreciate the propriety of subjects on which to expend it; as, to one who has over-lived, all values are the same, because nothing, and indifferent; while the other, from among the "roughs," is morbid from overgrowth, and likewise prodigal of its thought-treasure, because it has so much that it can afford to throw it away on everything, and considers all things that are, as equally worth gilding. The subject of MAUD is nothing — a mere commonplace incident, but artistically dealt with — a blanched, decayed sea-shell, around which the amber has gathered; and that of the newer poem is equally nothing, blades of sea-grass amber-cemented. Both are characterized by the extreme of affectation of suggestiveness — piers of thought being given, over which the reader must throw his own arches. Both are bold, defiant of laws which attempt to regulate forms, and of those which *should* regulate essences. Maud is irreligious through mental disease, produced by excess of sentimental action — "Leaves of Grass," through irregularly-developed mental action and insufficiency of sentiment. A calmer perception of Nature would have cor-

---

* "Maud and other Poems," by Alfred Tennyson. Ticknor & Fields, Boston.
† "Leaves of Grass." Brooklyn, N. Y.

rected in Tennyson that feeling which looks upon sorrow as the only thing poetic, and serenity and holy trust as things to which love has no alliance; while a higher seeing of nature would have shown Walt Whitman that all things in nature are not alike beautiful, or to be loved and honored by song.

Although it is mainly with the art of the two poems that we have to deal, the form rather than the motive, yet so entirely does the former arise from the latter, that the criticism passed on the one must lie upon the other. In the mere versification, for instance, of both, see what indifference to the dignity of verse (while there is still the extorted homage to its forms), arising in both cases, it would seem, from an overweening confidence in the value of what is said, as in the following passages:

> " Long have I sighed for a calm ; God grant I may find it at last!
> It will never be broken by Maud, she has neither savor nor salt,
> But a cold, clear, cut face, as I found when her carriage past,
> Perfectly beautiful: let it be granted her: where is the fault ? "
> *Maud*, Sec. ii., St. 1.

> " Do you suspect death? If I were to suspect death, I should die now.
> Do you think I could walk pleasantly and well-suited toward annihilation?
>
> Pleasantly and well-suited I walk,
> Whither I walk I cannot define, but I know it is good.
> The whole universe indicates that it is good.
> The past and present indicate that it is good." *Leaves of Grass*, p. 69.

All Tennyson's exquisite care over his lines produces no other impression than that which Walt Whitman's carelessness arrives at; viz., nonchalance with regard to forms. In either case, it is an imperfection, we are bold to say, since we do not love beauty and perfection of form for nothing, nor can the measure of poetic feeling be full when we do not care for the highest grace and symmetry of construction. It is an impertinence which says to us, "my ideas are so fine that they need no dressing up," even greater than that which says, "mine are so fine that they cannot be dressed as well as they deserve.". The child-like instinct demands perfect melody as an essential to perfect poetry, and more than that, the melodious thought will work out its just and adequate form by the essential law of its spiritual organization — when the heart sings, the feet will move to its music. An unjust measure in verse is *prima facie* evidence of a jarring note in the soul of the poem, and studied or permitted irregularity of form proves an arrogant self-estimation or irreverence in the poet; and both these poems are irreverent, irreligious, in fact. Maud commences, singularly enough, with the words, "I hate," and the whole sentiment of the poem ignores the nobler and purer feelings of humanity — it is full of hatred and morbid feeling, diseased from pure worldliness. This is well enough for one whom the world calls a laureate, but the true poet seeks a laurel that the world cannot gather, growing on mountains where its feet never tread ; he lives with beauty and things holy, or, if evil things come to him, it is that they may be commanded behind him. "Maud" rambles and raves through human love and human hate, and the hero lives his life of selfish desire and selfish enjoyment, and then through the bitterness of selfish regret and despair, without one thought of anything better than himself — the summit of creation. He worships nothing, even reverences nothing, his love is only passion, and his only thought of God one of fear. In his happiness, he is a cynic, in his unhappiness, a madman.

> "For the drift of the Maker is dark, an Isis hid by the veil.
> Who knows the ways of the world, how God will bring them about?
> Our planet is one, the suns are many, the world is wide.
> Shall I weep if a Poland fall? shall I shriek if a Hungary fall?
> Or an infant civilization be ruled with rod or with knout?
> I have not made the world, and He that made it will guide.
>
> Be mine a philosopher's life in the quiet woodland ways,
> Where if I cannot be gay let a passionless peace be my lot,
> Far off from the clamor of liars belied in the hubbub of lies;
> From the long-necked geese of the world that are ever hissing dispraise,
> Because their natures are little, and, whether he heed it or not,
> Where each man walks with his head in a cloud of poisonous flies.
>
> .   .   .   .
>
> Dead, long dead,
> Long dead!
> And my heart is a handful of dust,
> And the wheels go over my head,
> And my bones are shaken with pain,
> For into a shallow grave they are thrust,
> Only a yard beneath the street,
> And the hoofs of the horses beat, beat,
> The hoofs of the horses beat,
> Beat into my scalp and my brain,
> With never an end to the stream of passing feet,
> Driving, hurrying, marrying, burying,
> Clamor and rumble, and ringing and clatter,
> And here beneath it is all as bad,
> For I thought the dead had peace, but it is not so;
> To have no peace in the grave, is that not sad?
> But up and down and to and fro,
> Ever about me the dead men go;
> And then to hear a dead man chatter
> Is enough to drive one mad.
>
> Wretchedest age since Time began,
> They cannot even bury a man;
> And though we paid our tithes in the days that are gone,
> Not a bell was rung, not a prayer was read;
> It is that which makes us loud in the world of the dead;
> There is none that does his work, not one;
> A touch of their office might have sufficed,
> But the churchmen fain would kill their church,
> As the churches have killed their Christ.
>
> See, there is one of us sobbing,
> No limit to his distress;
> And another, a lord of all things, praying
> To his own great self, as I guess;
> And another a statesman there, betraying
> His party-secret, fool, to the press;
> And yonder a vile physician, blabbing
> The case of his patient — all for what?
> To tickle the maggot born in an empty head,

> And wheedle a world that loves him not,
> For it is but a world of the dead."

"Leaves of Grass" is irreligious, because it springs from a low recognition of the nature of Deity, not, perhaps, so in intent, but really so in its result. To Walt Whitman, all things are alike good — no thing is better than another, and thence there is no ideal, no aspiration, no progress to things better. It is not enough that all things are good, all things are *equally* good, and, therefore, there is no order in creation; no better, no worse — but all is a democratic level, from which can come no symmetry, in which there is no head, no subordination, no system, and, of course, no result. With a wonderful vigor of thought and intensity of perception, a power, indeed, not often found, "Leaves of Grass" has no ideality, no concentration, no purpose — it is barbarous, undisciplined, like the poetry of a half-civilized people, and, as a whole, useless, save to those miners of thought who prefer the metal in its unworked state. The preface of the book contains an inestimable wealth of this unworked ore — it is a creed of the material, not denying the ideal, but ignorant of it:

"The greatest poet hardly knows pettiness or triviality. If he breathes into anything that was before thought small, it dilates with the grandeur and life of the universe. He is a seer . . . he is individual . . . he is complete in himself . . . the others are as good as he, only he sees it and they do not. He is not one of the chorus . . . he does not stop for any regulation: he is the president of regulation. What the eyesight does to the rest he does to the rest. Who knows the curious mystery of the eyesight? The other senses corroborate themselves, but this is removed from any proof but its own, and foreruns the identities of the spiritual world. A single glance of it mocks all the investigations of man, and all the instruments and books of the earth, and all reasoning. What is marvellous? what is unlikely? what is impossible, or baseless, or vague? after you have once just opened the space of a peachpit, and given audience to far and near, and to the sunset, and had all things enter with electric swiftness, softly and duly, without confusion, or jostling, or jam.

"The land and sea, the animals, fishes, and birds, the sky of heaven and the orbs, the forests, mountains, and rivers, are not small themes . . . but folks expect of the poet to indicate more than the beauty and dignity which always attach to dumb, real objects . . . they expect him to indicate the path between reality and their souls. Men and women perceive the beauty well enough . . . probably as well as he. The passionate tenacity of hunters, woodmen, early risers, cultivators of gardens and orchards and fields, the love of healthy women for the manly form, sea-faring persons, drivers of horses, the passion for light and the open air, all is an old varied sign of the unfailing perception of beauty, and of a residence of the poetic in out-door people. They can never be assisted by poets to perceive . . . some may, but they never can. The poetic quality is not marshalled in rhyme, or uniformity, or abstract addresses to things, nor in melancholy complaints or good precepts, but is the life of these and much else, and is in the soul. The profit of rhyme is that it drops seeds of a sweeter and more luxuriant rhyme; and of uniformity, that it conveys itself into its own roots in the ground out of sight. The rhyme and uniformity of perfect poems show the free growth of metrical laws, and bud from them as unerringly and loosely as lilacs or roses on a bush, and take shapes as compact as the shapes of chestnuts, and oranges, and melons, and pears, and shed the perfume impalpable to form. The fluency and ornaments of the finest poems, or music, or orations, or recitations, are not independent, but dependent. All beauty comes from beautiful blood and a beautiful brain. If the greatnesses are in conjunction in a man or woman it is enough . . the fact will prevail through the universe . . . but the gaggery and gilt of a million

2

years will not prevail. Who troubles himself about his ornaments or fluency is lost."

   .   .   .   .

"The greatest poet has less a marked style, and is more the channel of thoughts and things without increase or diminution, and is the free channel of himself. He swears to his art. I will not be meddlesome, I will not have in my writing any elegance, or effect, or originality, to hang in the way between me and the rest, like curtains. I will have nothing hang in the way, not the richest curtains. What I tell, I tell for precisely what it is. Let who may exalt, or startle, or fascinate, or soothe, I will have purposes as health, or heat, or snow, has, and be as regardless of observation. What I experience or portray shall go from my composition without a shred of my composition. You shall stand by my side, and look in the mirror with me."

"I am of old and young, of the foolish as much as the wise,
Regardless of others, ever regardful of others,
Maternal as well as paternal, a child as well as a man,
Stuffed with the stuff that is coarse, and stuffed with the stuff that is fine,
One of the great nation, the nation of many nations — the smallest the same and the largest the same.
A southerner soon as a northerner, a planter nonchalant and hospitable,
A Yankee bound my own way . . . ready for trade . . . my joints the limberest joints on earth and the sternest joints on earth,
A Kentuckian walking the vale of the Elkhorn in my deerskin leggings,
A boatman over the lakes or bays or along coasts . . . a Hoosier, a Badger, a Buckeye,
A Louisianian or Georgian, a poke-easy from sandhills and pines,
At home on Kanadian snow-shoes or up in the bush, or with fishermen off Newfoundland,
At home in the fleet of ice-boats, sailing with the rest and tacking,
At home on the hills of Vermont or in the woods of Maine or the Texan ranch,
Comrade of Californians . . . comrade of free northwesterners, loving their big proportions,
Comrade of raftsmen and coalmen — comrade of all who shake hands and welcome to drink and meat;
A learner with the simplest, a teacher of the thoughtfullest,
A novice beginning experient of myriads of seasons,
Of every hue and trade and rank, of every caste and religion,
Not merely of the New World but of Africa, Europe or Asia . . . a wandering savage,
A farmer, mechanic, or artist, . . . a gentleman, sailor, lover, or quaker,
A prisoner, fancy-man, rowdy, lawyer, physician, or priest.

   .   .   .   .

I am he attesting sympathy;
Shall I make my list of things in the house, and skip the house that supports them?
I am the poet of common sense, and of the demonstrable, and of immortality;
And am not the poet of goodness only . . . I do not decline to be the poet of wickedness also.

Washes and razors for foofoos, . . . for me freckles and a bristling beard.

What blurt is it about virtue and about vice?
Evil propels me, and reform of evil propels me . . . I stand indifferent,
My gait is no fault-finder's or rejecter's gait,
I moisten the roots of all that has grown."

In other words, according to Walt Whitman's theory, the greatest poet is he who performs the office of camera to the world, merely reflecting what he sees — art is merely reproduction.

Yet it cannot be denied that he has felt the beauty of the material in full measure, and sometimes most felicitously.

"A child said, What is the grass? fetching it to me with full hands;
How could I answer the child? . . . I do not know what it is any more than he.

I guess it must be the flag of my disposition out of hopeful green stuff woven.

Or I guess it is the handkerchief of the Lord,
A scented gift aud remembrancer designedly dropped,
Bearing the owner's name someway in the corners, that we may see and remark,
      and say, Whose?

Or I guess the grass is itself a child . . . the produced babe of the vegetation.

Or I guess it is a uniform hieroglyphic,
And it means, Sprouting alike in broad zones and narrow zones,
Growing among black folks as among white,
Kanuck, Tuckahoe, Congressmen, Cuff, I give them the same, I receive them
      the same.

And now it seems to me the beautiful uncut hair of graves.

     .   .   .   .

The big doors of the country-barn stand open and ready,
The dried grass of the harvest-time loads the slow-drawn wagon,
The clear light plays on the brown gray and green intertinged,
The armfuls are packed to the sagging mow:
I am there . . . I help . . . I came stretched atop of the load,
I felt its soft jolts . . . one leg reclined on the other,
I jump from the crossbeams, and seize the clover and timothy,
And roll head over heels, and tangle my hair full of wisps.

     .   .   .   .

I think I could turn and live a while with the animals . . . they are so placid
      and self-contained,
I stand and look at them sometimes half the day long.

They do not sweat and whine about their condition,
They do not lie awake in the dark and weep for their sins,
They do not make me sick discussing their duty to God,
Not one is dissatisfied . . . not one is demented with the mania of owning
      things,
Not one kneels to another nor to his kind that lived thousands of years ago,
Not one is respectable or industrious over the whole earth.

So they show their relations to me and I accept them;
They bring me tokens of myself . . . they evince them plainly in their pos-
      session.

     .   /   .   .   .   .   .   .

When the dull nights are over, and the dull days also,
When the soreness of lying so much in bed is over,
When the physician, after long putting off, gives the silent and terrible look for
      an answer,
When the children come hurried and weeping, and the brothers and sisters have
      been sent for,
When medicines stand unused on the shelf, and the camphor-smell has per-
      vaded the rooms,
When the faithful hand of the living does not desert the hand of the dying,
When the twitching lips press lightly on the forehead of the dying,
When the breath ceases and the pulse of the heart ceases,
Then the corpse-limbs stretch on the bed, and the living look upon them,
They are palpable as the living are palpable.

The living look upon the corpse with their eyesight,
But without eyesight lingers a different living and looks curiously on the corpse.

     .   .   .   .

I knew a man, . . . he was a common farmer, . . . he was the father of five
      sons, . . . and in them were the fathers of sons, . . . and in them were the
      fathers of sons.

This man was of wonderful vigor and calmness and beauty of person;
The shape of his head, the richness and breadth of his manners, the pale yellow
      and white of his hair and beard, the immeasurable meaning of his black
      eyes,
These I used to go and visit him to see. . . . He was wise also,
He was six feet tall, . . . he was over eighty years old, . . . his sons were mas-
      sive, clean, bearded, tanfaced, and handsome,
They and his daughters loved him, . . . all who saw him loved him, ...they
      did not love him by allowance, . . . they loved him with personal love;

He drank water only, . . . the blood shone like scarlet through the clear brown
skin of his face;
He was a frequent gunner and fisher. . . . he sailed his boat himself, . . . he had
a fine one presented to him by a shipjoiner, . . . he had fowling pieces,
presented to him by men that loved him;
When he went with his five sons and many grandsons to hunt or fish you would
pick him out as the most beautiful and vigorous of the gang,
You would wish long and long to be with him, . . . you would wish to sit by
him in the boat that you and he might touch each other."

· · · · · · · · · · ·

It is not possible to compare the feverish, dying sentiment of
Tennyson, dying from false indulgence, to the rude, vigorous,
and grand if chaotic thought of Walt Whitman, imperfect only
from want of development — the poems are alike maimed, but
one from loss of parts, the other from not yet having attained
its parts. But still they are the extremes — truth lies between
them always. What if Columbus had sailed round the world,
and made its extremes meet? He would only have been back
in Spain again — the true end of his voyage was midway.

From the New York Daily Times, (1856.)

LEAVES OF GRASS, — Brooklyn, N. Y. — 1856.

What Centaur have we here, half man, half beast, neighing
defiance to all the world? What conglomerate of thought is
this before us, with insolence, philosophy, tenderness, blasphe-
my, beauty and gross indecency tumbling in drunken confusion
through the pages? Who is this arrogant young man who proclaims himself the Poet of the Time, and who roots like a pig
among a rotten garbage of licentious thoughts? Who is this
flushed and full-blooded lover of Nature who studies her so
affectionately, and who sometimes utters her teachings with a
lofty tongue? This mass of extraordinary contradictions, this
fool and this wise man, this lover of beauty and this sunken
sensualist, this original thinker and blind egotist, is Mr. WALT
WHITMAN, author of *Leaves of Grass,* and, according to his
own account, " a Kosmos."
Some time since there was left at the office of this paper a
thin quarto volume bound in green and gold. On opening the
book we first beheld, as a frontispiece, the picture of a man in
his shirt sleeves, wearing an expression of settled arrogance
upon his countenance. We next arrived at a title page of mag-
nificent proportions, with letter-press at least an inch and a half
in length. From this title page we learned that the book was
entitled *Leaves of Grass,* and was printed at Brooklyn in the
year 1855. This inspected, we passed on to what seemed to be
a sort of preface, only that it had no beginning, was remarkable
for a singular sparseness in the punctuation, and was broken up
in a confusing manner by frequent rows of dots separating the

paragraphs. To this succeeded eighty-two pages of what appeared at the first glance to be a number of prose sentences printed somewhat after a biblical fashion. Almost at the first page we opened we lighted upon the confession that the author was

"WALT WHITMAN, an American, one of the roughs,
a Kosmos,
Disorderly, fleshy and sensual...."

This was sufficient basis for a theory. We accordingly arrived at the conclusion that the insolent-looking young man on the frontispiece was this same WALT WHITMAN, and author of the *Leaves of Grass*.

Then returning to the fore-part of the book, we found proof slips of certain review articles written about the *Leaves of Grass*. One of these purported to be extracted from a periodical entitled the *United States Review*, the other was headed "From the *American Phrenological Journal*." These were accompanied by a printed copy of an extravagant letter of praise addressed by Mr. RALPH WALDO EMERSON to Mr. WALT WHITMAN, complimenting him on the benefaction conferred on society in the present volume. On subsequently comparing the critiques from the *United States Review* and the *Phrenological Journal* with the preface of the *Leaves of Grass*, we discovered unmistakable internal evidence that Mr. WALT WHITMAN, true to his character as a Kosmos, was not content with writing a book, but was also determined to review it; so Mr. WALT WHITMAN, had concocted both those criticisms of his own work, treating it we need not say how favorably. This little discovery of our "disorderly" acquaintance's mode of proceeding rather damped any enthusiasm with which Mr. EMERSON's extravagant letter may have inspired us. We reflected, here is a man who sets himself up as the poet and teacher of his time; who professes a scorn of everything mean and dastardly, and double-faced, who hisses with scorn as he passes one in the street whom he suspects of the taint, hypocrisy — yet this self-contained teacher, this rough-and-ready scorner of dishonesty, this rowdy knight-errant who tilts against all lies and shams, himself perpetrates a lie and a sham at the very outset of his career. It is a lie to write a review of one's own book, then extract it out from the work in which it appeared and send it out to the world as an impartial editorial utterance. It is an act that the most degraded helot of literature might blush to commit. It is a dishonesty committed against one's own nature, and all the world. Mr. WALT WHITMAN in one of his candid rhapsodies announces that he is "no more modest than immodest." Perhaps in literary matters he carries the theory farther, and is no more honest than dishonest. He likewise says in his preface: "The great poets are known by the absence in them of tricks, and by the justification of perfect personal candor." Where, then, can we place Mr. WALT WHITMAN'S claims upon immortality?

We confess we turn from Mr. WHITMAN as Critic, to Mr. WHITMAN as Poet, with considerable pleasure. We prefer occupying that independent position which Mr. WHITMAN claims for man, and forming our own opinions, rather than swallowing those ready-made. This gentleman begins his poetic life with a coarse and bitter scorn of the past. We have been living stale and unprofitable lives; we have been surfeited with luxury and high living, and are grown lethargic and dull; the age is fast decaying, when, lo! the trump of the Angel Whitman brings the dead to life, and animates the slumbering world. If we obey the dictates of that trumpet, we will do many strange things. We will fling off all moral clothing and walk naked over the earth. We will disembarrass our language of all the proprieties of speech, and talk indecency broadcast. We will act in short as if the Millenium were arrived in this our present day, when the absence of all vice would no longer necessitate a virtuous discretion. We fear much, Mr. WALT WHITMAN, that the time is not yet come for the nakedness of purity. We are not yet virtuous enough to be able to read your poetry aloud to our children and our wives. What might be pastoral simplicity five hundred years hence, would perhaps be stigmatized as the coarsest indecency now, and — we regret to think that you have spoken too soon.

The adoration of the "Me," the "Ego," the "eternal and universal I," to use the jargon of the Boston Oracle, is the prevailing motive of *Leaves of Grass*. Man embraces and comprehends the whole. He is everything, and everything is him. All nature ebbs and flows through him in ceaseless tides. He is "his own God and his own Devil," and everything that he does is good. He rejoices with all who rejoice; suffers with all who suffer. This doctrine is exemplified in the book by a panorama as it were of pictures, each of which is shared in by the author, who belongs to the universe, as the universe belongs to him. In detailing these pictures he hangs here and there shreds and tassels of his wild philosophy, till his work, like a maniac's robe, is bedizened with fluttering tags of a thousand colors. With all his follies, insolence, and indecency, no modern poet that we know of has presented finer descriptive passages than Mr. WALT WHITMAN. His phrasing, and the strength and completeness of his epithets, are truly wonderful. He paints in a single line with marvellous power and comprehensiveness. The following rhapsody will illustrate his fulness of epithet:

"I am he that walks with the tender and growing night;
I call to the earth and sea, half held by the night.

"Press close bare-bosomed night! Press close magnetic, nourishing night!
Night of South winds! Night of the large few stars!
Still nodding night! Mad, naked, Summer night!

*Smile, O voluptuous cool-breathed earth!
Earth of the slumbering and liquid trees!
Earth of departed sunset! Earth of the mountains misty-topt!
Earth of the vitreous pour of the full moon just tinged with blue!
Earth of shine and dark, mottling the tide of the river!
Earth of the limpid gray of clouds brighter and clearer for my sake!
Far-swooping elbowed earth! Rich apple-blossomed earth!
Smile, for your lover comes!

" You sea! I resign myself to you also . . . . I guess what you mean,
I behold from the beach your crooked inviting fingers,
I believe you refuse to go back without feeling of me;
We must have a turn together . . . . I undress . . . . hurry me out of sight of the
    land.
Cushion me soft . . . . *rock me in billowy drowse,*
Dash me with amorous wet. . . . I can repay you.

" Sea of stretched ground-swells!
Sea, breathing broad and convulsive breaths!
Sea of the brine of life! *Sea of unshovelled and always ready graves!*
Howler and scooper of storms! Capricious and dainty sea!
I am integral with you . . . . I too am of one phase and of all phases."

Here are fine expressions well placed. Mr. WHITMAN's
study of nature has been close and intense. He has expressed
certain things better than any other man who has gone before
him. He talks well, and largely, and tenderly of sea and sky,
and men and trees, and women and children. His observation
and his imagination are both large and well-developed. Take
this picture; how pathetic, how tenderly touched!

" Agonies are one of my changes of garments;
I do not ask the wounded person how he feels . . . . I myself become the
    wounded person,
My hurt turns livid upon me as I lean on a cane and observe.

" I am the mashed fireman with breast-bone broken . . . . tumbling walls buried
    me in their debris,
Heat and smoke I inspired . . . . I heard the yelling shouts of my comrades,
I heard the distant click of their picks and shovels;
They have cleared the beams away . . . . they tenderly lift me forth.

" I lie in the night air in my red shirt . . . . the pervading hush is for my sake,
Painless after all I lie, exhausted but not so unhappy.
White and beautiful are the faces around me . . . . the heads are bared of their
    fire-caps.
The kneeling crowd fades with the light of the torches."

If it were permitted to us to outrage all precedent, and print
that which should not be printed, we could cull some passages
from the " Leaves of Grass," and place them in strange con-
trast with the extracts we have already made. If being a Kosmos is to set no limits to one's imagination; to use coarse epithets when coarseness is not needful; to roam like a drunken
satyr, with inflamed blood, through every field of lascivious
thought; to return time after time with a seemingly exhaustless prurient pleasure to the same licentious phrases and ideas,
and to jumble all this up with bits of marvellously beautiful description, exquisite touches of nature, fragments of savagely-
uttered truth, shreds of unleavened philosophy; if to do all this
is to be a Kosmos, then indeed we cede to Mr. WALT WHITMAN

his arrogated title. Yet it seems to us that one may be profound
without being beastly; one may teach philosophy without clothing it in slang; one may be a great poet without using a language which shall outlaw the minstrel from every decent hearth.
Mr. WALT WHITMAN does not think so. He tears the veil from
all that society by a well-ordered law shrouds in a decent mystery. He is proud of his nakedness of speech; he glories in his
savage scorn of decorum. Like the priests of Belus, he wreathes
around his brow the emblems of the Phallic worship.

   With all this muck of abomination soiling the pages, there is
a wondrous, unaccountable fascination about the *Leaves of
Grass*. As we read it again and again, and we will confess
that we have returned to it often, a singular order seems to arise
out of its chaotic verses. Out of the mire and slough edged
thoughts and keen philosophy start suddenly, as the men of
Cadmus sprang from the muddy loam. A lofty purpose still
dominates the uncleanness and the ridiculous self-conceit in
which the author, led astray by ignorance, indulges. He gives
token everywhere that he is a huge uncultivated thinker. No
country save this could have given birth to the man. His mind
is Western — brawny, rough, and original. Wholly uncultivated, and beyond his associates, he has begotten within him
the egotism of intellectual solitude. Had he mingled with
scholars and men of intellect, those effete beings whom he so
despises, he would have learned much that would have been
beneficial. When we have none of our own size to measure
ourselves with, we are apt to fancy ourselves broader and taller
than we are. The poet of the little country town, who has
reigned for years the Virgil or Anacreon of fifty square miles,
finds, when he comes into the great metropolis, that he has not
had all the thinking to himself. There he finds hundreds of men
who have thought the same things as himself, and uttered them
more fully. He is astonished to discover that his intellectual
language is limited, when he thought that he had fathomed
expression. He finds his verse unpolished, his structure defec-
tive, his best thoughts said before. He enters into the strife,
clashes with his fellows, measures swords with this one, gives
thrust for thrust with the other, until his muscles harden and
his frame swells. He looks back upon his provincial intellectual existence with a smile; he laughs at his country arrogance
and ignorant faith in himself. Now we gather from Mr. WHIT-
MAN'S own admissions — admissions that assume the form of
boasts — that he has mingled but little with intellectual men.
The love of the physical — which is the key-note of his entire
book — has as yet altogether satisfied him. To mix with large-
limbed, clean-skinned men, to look on ruddy, fair-proportioned
women, is his highest social gratification. This love of the
beautiful is by him largely and superbly expressed in many

places, and it does one good to read those passages pulsating
with the pure blood of animal life. But those associates, though
manly and handsome, help but little to a man's inner appreciation of himself. Perhaps our author among his comrades had
no equal in intellectual force. He reigned triumphantly in an
unquestioning circle of admirers. How easy, then, to fancy
one's self a wonderful being! How easy to look around and
say, "There are none like me here. I am the coming man!"
It may be said that books will teach such a man the existence
of other powerful minds, but this will not do. Such communion
is abstract, and has but little force. It is only in the actual com-
bat of mind striving with mind that a man comes properly to
estimate himself. Mr. WHITMAN has grown up in an intellectual isolation which has fully developed all the eccentricities of
his nature. He has made some foolish theory that to be rough
is to be original. Now, external softness of manner is in no
degree incompatible with muscularity of intellect; and one
thinks no more of a man's brains for his treading on one's toes
without an apology, or his swearing in the presence of women.
When Mr. WHITMAN shall have learned that a proper worship
of the individual man need not be expressed so as to seem insolence, and that men are not to be bullied into receiving as a
Messiah every man who sneers at them in his portrait, and dis-
gusts them in his writings, we have no doubt that in some chas-
tened mood of mind he will produce moving and powerful books.
We select some passages exhibiting the different phases of Mr.
WHITMAN'S character. We do so more readily as, from the
many indecencies contained in *Leaves of Grass*, we do not believe it will find its way into many families.

A MODEST PROFESSION OF FAITH.

"Nothing, not God, is greater to one than one's self is,
    And whoever walks a furlong without sympathy, walks to his own funeral,
    Dressed in his shroud."

A FINE LANDSCAPE.

" The turbid pool that lies in the Autumn forest,
    The moon that descends the steeps of the soughing twilight,
    Toss, sparkles of day and dusk . . . . toss on the black stems that decay in the
        muck;
    Toss to the moaning gibberish of the dry limbs."

A TRUTH.

" I, too, am not a bit tamed . . . . I, too, am untranslatable;
    I sound my barbaric yawp over the roofs of the world."

A DEATH-BED.

" When the dull nights are over, and the dull days also;
    When the soreness of lying so much in bed is over,
    When the physician, after long putting off, gives the silent and terrible look for
        an answer;
    When the children come hurried and weeping, and the brothers and sisters
        have been sent for;
    When medicines stand unused on the shelf, and the camphor-smell has
        pervaded the rooms;

When the faithful hand of the living does not desert the hand of the dying;
When the twitching lips press lightly on the forehead of the dying;
When the breath ceases, and the pulse of the heart ceases;
Then the corpse limbs stretch on the bed, and the living look upon them,
They are palpable as the living are palpable.
The living look upon the corpse with their eye-sight,
But without eye-sight lingers a different living and looks curiously on the corpse."

IMMORTALITY.

' If maggots and ruts ended us, then suspicion, and treachery and death.
Do you suspect death? If I were to suspect death I should die now.
Do you think I could walk pleasantly and well-suited towards annihilation ? "

THE REVOLUTION OF 1848.

" Yet behind all, lo, a shape,
Vague as the night, draped interminably, head, front and form in scarlet folds,
Whose face and eyes none may see,
Out of its robes only this . . . . the red robes lifted by the arm,
One finger pointed high over the top, like the head of a snake appears.

" Meanwhile corpses lie in new-made graves . . . . bloody corpses of young men:
The rope of the gibbet, hangs heavily . . . . the bullets of princes are flying . . . .
        the creatures of power laugh aloud.
And all these things bear fruits . . . . and they are good.

" Those corpses of young men,
Those martyrs that hang from the gibbets . . . . those hearts pierced by the gray
        lead,
Cold and motionless as they seem . . . . live elsewhere with unslaughtered
        vitality.

" They live in other young men, O Kings,
They live in brothers again ready to defy you;
They were purified by death . . . . they were taught and exalted.

" *Not a grave of the murdered for freedom but sows seed for freedom . . . . in its
        turn to bear seed,
Which the winds carry afar and resow, and the rains and the snows nourish;
Not a disembodied spirit can the weapons of tyrants let loose,
But it stalks invisibly o'er the earth . . . . whispering, counselling, cautioning.*"

Since the foregoing was written — and it has been awaiting its turn at the printing press some months — Mr. WALT WHITMAN has published an enlarged edition of his works, from which it is fair to infer that his first has had a ready sale. From twelve poems, of which the original book was composed, he has brought the number up to thirty, all characterized by the same wonderful amalgamation of beauty and indecency. He has, however, been in his new edition guilty of a fresh immodesty. He has not alone printed Mr. EMERSON's private letter in an appendix, but he has absolutely printed a passage of that gentleman's note, " I greet you at the beginning of a great career," in gold letters on the back, and affixed the name of the writer. Now, Mr. EMERSON wrote a not very wise letter to Mr. WHITMAN on the publication of the first twelve poems — indorsing them ; and so there might be some excuse for the poet's anxiety to let the public know that his first edition was commended from such a quarter. But with the additional poems, Mr. EMERSON has certainly nothing whatever to do ; nevertheless, the same note that indorsed the twelve is used by Mr. WHITMAN in the coolest manner to indorse the thirty-two. This is making a private letter go very far indeed. It is as if after a man signed a deed, the person interested should introduce a number of additional clauses, making the original signature still cover them. It is a literary fraud, and Mr. WHITMAN ought to be ashamed of himself.

Still, this man has brave stuff in him. He is truly astonishing. The originality of his philosophy is of little account, for if it is truth, it must be ever the same, whether uttered by his lips or PLATO's. In manner only can we be novel, and truly Mr. WHITMAN is novelty itself. Since the greater portion of this review was written, we confess to having been attracted again and again to *Leaves of Grass.* It has a singular electric attraction. Its manly vigor, its brawny health, seem to incite and satisfy. We look forward with curious anticipation to Mr. WALT WHITMAN's future works.

———

A LETTER IMPROMPTU.

MY DEAR MR. ———

.   .   .   .

.   .   .   .

But you have a native in Brooklyn, a poet, fire-eyed and large-
    hearted,
Who belongs to the ancient and elder, the rough-hewn, real .
    immortals —
Those wise old gods, whose faces laugh out in the red light of
    morning,
The fresh, dewy light of the morning, when man was youthful,
    and nature;
He, Walt Whitman, a "rough," old Cosmos, primeval diurnal,
Unwieldy as any Behemoth, trampling mud-swamps Nilotic,
Though trampling to life the Lotus, and wise old serpent of
    Egypt;
Graceful as fawns and panthers, full of the marrow of ripe men,
Luscious as grapes and roses, with thoughts like the breath of
    the violet,
He, the fresh comer, new speaker, trying no scholars' hex-
    ameters,
Has faith that the prose-tongue can serve him, and seizing the
    rough words,
Such as he finds them spoken by brother and sister Manhattans,
Sets them to sweeter and deeper music than ears heard afore-
    time;
This is the man and the measure dearer to me than all others,
Dearer by far than ——— ———, than mongrel musical
    singers, —

He is not afraid — Walt Whitman — to speak the things that
    he thinketh,
To speak of himself and his feelings, his innermost, privatest
    feelings.
Poet, and soul representative, knows that he stands for his
    fellows ;
Knows that the person is sacred, the person, the passions, the
    organs.
Is not afraid to sing of the love of a man for a woman ;
Daring, he lifts up the veil, exposing the wonderful process ;
Sings of its rosy-lipped kisses, its ravishing surfeiting blisses,
The storm of its rapture and madness, the prostrate repose of
    its calm.
Careth he naught for the saints, careth he naught for the
    sinners.
He is a saint and a sinner — a man with his feelings about him ;
Alive in the world of to-day — not to be shuffled nor cheated
Out of his rights as a man, out of his loves for a woman.
Sees nothing common about him, nothing that is not poetic ;
Sees in the shops of the city — the trade, the commerce, the
    caucus,
Sees in the everyday life of worker, dandy, and loafer,
Mysterious things and dramatic, wonder-worlds lying beneath
    them.
Is not ashamed of mechanics as friends of his and companions.
This is the new Yankee poet, this is the man for my money !
Who in his box of a body carries the race and its burdens,
Its joys, its sorrows and laughters, its antics, follies and
    wisdom ;
Carries the wealth of its towns, its arts, its science and
    knowledge,
Carries the love of the sexes, the beauty of God and the
    universe.
So I call to all Yankee-land, Come up and see your new poet !
He who has broke from the temple, broke from the old Eastern
    temple,
Trampled the fire of its altars — leaving its albs and its crosiers,
Its cowls and garlands and song robes, standing here in the
    West-land,
Free as the forest winds, and bold as the Rocky Mountains,
Clad in the robes of the prairies — seeking to build up a new
    one.
Him with his perfect faith, and his wild, barbaric "yawps"
    which he
Flings with an ominous thunder over the "roofs" of the Old
    World,
Him seeks the Western genius seized for the first time in
    earnest,

Making him "landlord and sealord, airlord," and starlord and
    master :
Such as I think him 's Walt Whitman — Walt Whitman, *essentially* Walt !
Not such as at present he shows him in his wonderful "Grass
    Leaves."
For this is the grand epileptic oracular outburst he utters,
In the first grip of the god taking possession within him.
But if he be true to himself, to the god, and to art, our divinest
Symbol of meaning and beauty which man has discovered in
    this world,
He is the Titan you speak of, out of whose loins there shall
    issue
The fiery brood of Americans, running their errands of love up
The sides of the high western mountains — greatest of men
    and of heroes !
But pray do not think I despise the ⸺ ⸺ ⸺
Nor yet the young lady hexameters, of mongrel musical singers.
I see from what depths it proceedeth — the ⸺ ⸺ ⸺
I see in what shallows it runneth — the musical babble
    of ⸺
I 'm thankful for something in one case; thankful for nothing
    in t' other.
    Chelsea, Mass., 1857.   JANUARY SEARLE.

From the London Weekly Dispatch. (*London, England*, 1856.)

LEAVES OF GRASS. By Walt Whitman. Horsell, Oxford Street.

We have before us one of the most extraordinary specimens
of Yankee intelligence and American eccentricity in author-
ship it is possible to conceive. It is of a *genus* so peculiar as
to embarass us, and has an air at once so novel, so audacious,
and so strange, as to verge upon absurdity, and yet it would
be an injustice to pronounce it so, as the work is saved from
this extreme by a certain mastery over diction not very easy of
definition. What Emerson has pronounced to be good must
not be lightly treated, and before we pronounce upon the merits of this performance it is but right to examine them. We
have, then, a series of pithy prose sentences strung together —
forming twelve grand divisions in all, but which, having a rude
rhythmical cadence about them, admit of the designation poetical being applied. They are destitute of rhyme, measure of
feet, and the like, every condition under which poetry is generally understood to exist being absent; but in their strength of
expression, their fervor, hearty wholesomeness, their originality, mannerism, and freshness, one finds in them a singular har-

mony and flow, as if by reading, they gradually formed themselves into melody, and adopted characteristics peculiar and
appropriate to themselves alone. If, however, some sentences
be fine, there are others altogether laughable ; nevertheless, in
the bare strength, the unhesitating frankness of a man who " believes in the flesh and the appetites," and who dares to call simplest things by their plainest names, conveying also a large
sense of the beautiful, and with an emphasis which gives a
clearer conception of what manly modesty really is than any
thing we have, in all conventional forms of word, deed, or act
so far known of, that we rid ourselves, little by little, of the
strangeness with which we greet this bluff new-comer, and beginning to understand him better, appreciate him in proportion
as he becomes more known. He will soon make his way into
the confidence of his readers, and his poems in time will become
a pregnant text-book, out of which quotations as sterling as the
minted gold will be taken and applied to every form and phase
of the " inner " or the " outer " life ; and we express our plea-
ure in making the acquaintance of Walt Whitman, hoping to
know more of him in time to come.

From the Brooklyn Daily Times. (1856.)

LEAVES OF GRASS.   A volume of Poems, just published.

To give judgment on real poems, one needs an account of the
poet himself. Very devilish to some, and very divine to some,
will appear the poet of these new poems, the " LEAVES OF
GRASS ; " an attempt, as they are, of a naïve, masculine, affectionate, contemplative, sensual, imperious person, to cast into
literature not only his own grit and arrogance, but his own -
flesh and form, undraped, regardless of models, regardless of
modesty or law, and ignorant or silently scornful, as at first appears, of all except his own presence and experience, and all
outside the fiercely loved land of his birth, and the birth of his
parents, and their parents for several generations before him.
Politeness this man has none, and regulation he has none. A
rude child of the people ! — No imitation — No foreigner — but
a growth and idiom of America. No discontented — a careless
slouch, enjoying to-day. No dilettante democrat — a man who
is art-and-part with the commonalty, and with immediate life —
loves the streets — loves the docks — loves the free rasping talk
of men — likes to be called by his given name, and nobody at
all need Mr. him — can laugh with laughers — likes the ungen-
teel ways of laborers — is not prejudiced one mite against the
Irish — talks readily with them — talks readily with niggers —
does not make a stand on being a gentleman, nor on learning

or manners — eats cheap fare, likes the strong flavored coffee of the coffee-stands in the market, at sunrise — likes a supper of oysters fresh from the oyster-smack — likes to make one at the crowded table among sailors and work-people — would leave a select soiree of elegant people any time to go with tumultuous men, roughs, receive their caresses and welcome, listen to their noise, oaths, smut, fluency, laughter, repartee — and can preserve his presence perfectly among these, and the like of these. The effects he produces in his poems are no effects of artists or the arts, but effects of the original eye or arm, or the actual atmosphere, or tree, or bird. You may feel the unconscious teaching of a fine brute, but will never feel the artificial teaching of a fine writer or speaker.

Other poets celebrate great events, personages, romances, wars, loves, passions, the victories and power of their country, or some real or imagined incident — and polish their work, and come to conclusions, and satisfy the reader. This poet celebrates natural propensities in himself; and that is the way he celebrates all. He comes to no conclusions, and does not satisfy the reader. He certainly leaves him what the serpent left the woman and the man, the taste of the Paradisaic tree of the knowledge of good and evil, never to be erased again.

What good is it to argue about egotism? There can be no two thoughts on Walt Whitman's egotism. That is avowedly ' what he steps out of the crowd and turns and faces them for. Mark, critics! Otherwise is not used for you the key that leads to the use of the other keys to this well-enveloped man. His whole work, his life, manners, friendships, writings, all have among their leading purposes an evident purpose to stamp a new type of character, namely his own, and indelibly fix it and publish it, not for a model but an illustration, for the present and future of American letters and American young men, for the south the same as the north, and for the Pacific and Mississippi country, and Wisconsin and Texas and Kansas and Canada and Havana and Nicaragua, just as much as New York and Boston. Whatever is needed toward this achievement he puts his hand to, and lets imputations take their time to die.

First be yourself what you would show in your poem — such seems to be this man's example and inferred rebuke to the schools of poets. He makes no allusions to books or writers; their spirits do not seem to have touched him; he has not a word to say for or against them, or their theories or ways. He never offers others; what he continually offers is the man whom our Brooklynites know so well. Of pure American breed, large and lusty — age thirty-six years, (1855,) — never once using medicine — never dressed in black, always dressed freely and clean in strong clothes — neck open, shirt-collar flat and broad, countenance tawny transparent red, beard well-mottled with white, hair like hay after it has been mowed in the field and lies tossed and streaked — his physiology corroborating a rugged phrenology * — a person singularly beloved and looked toward, especially by young men and the illiterate — one who has firm attachments there, and associates there — one who does not associate with literary people — a man never called upon to make speeches at public dinners — never on platforms amid the crowds of clergymen, or professors, or aldermen, or congressmen — rather down in the bay with pilots in their pilot-boat — or off on a cruise with fishers in a fishing-smack — or riding on a Broadway omnibus, side by side with the driver — or with a band of loungers over the open grounds of the country — fond of New York and Brooklyn — fond of the life of the great ferries — one whom, if you should meet, you need not expect to meet an extraordinary person — one in whom you will see the singularity which consists in no singularity — whose contact is no dazzle or fascination, nor requires any deference, but has the easy fascination of what is homely and accustomed — as of something you knew before, and was waiting for — there you have Walt Whitman, the begetter of a new offspring out of literature, taking with easy nonchalance the chances of its present reception, and, through all misunderstandings and distrusts, the chances of its future reception — preferring always to speak *for himself rather than have others speak for him.

From the Christian Spritualist. (1856.)

LEAVES OF GRASS.

Carlyle represents a contemporary reviewer taking leave of the Belles-Lettres department somewhat in this abrupt manner: "The end having come, it is fit that we end — Poetry having

---

* *Phrenological Notes on W. Whitman,* by L. N. Fowler, July, 1849. — Size of head large, 23 inches. Leading traits appear to be Friendship, Sympathy, Sublimity, and Self-Esteem, and markedly among his combinations the dangerous faults of Indolence, a tendency to the pleasures of Voluptuousness and Alimentiveness, and a certain reckless swing of animal will.

Amativeness large, *6; Philoprogenitiveness, 6: Adhesiveness, 6; Inhabitiveness, 6; Concentrativeness, 4; Combativeness, 6; Destructiveness, 5 to 6; Alimentiveness, 6: Acquisitiveness, 4: Secretiveness, 3; Cautiousness, 6: Approbativeness, 4: Self-Esteem, 6 to 7; Firmness, 6 to 7; Conscientiousness, 6: Hope, 4; Marvellousness, 3: Veneration, 4: Benevolence, 6 to 7; Constructiveness, 5: Ideality, 5 to 6; Sublimity, 6 to 7; Imitation, 5: Mirthfulness, 5; Individuality, 6; Form, 6; Size, 6; Weight, 6; Color, 3; Order, 5; Calculation, 5; Locality, 6; Eventuality, 6; Time, 3; Tune, 4; Language, 5; Causality, 5 to 6; Comparison, 6; Suavitiveness, 4; Intuitiveness, or Human Nature, 6.

---

* The organs are marked by figures from 1 to 7, indicating their degrees of development, 1 meaning very small, 2 small, 3 moderate, 4 average, 5 full, 6 large, and 7 very large.

ceased to be read, or published, or written, how can it continue to be reviewed? With your Lake Schools, and Border-Thief Schools, and Cockney and Satanic Schools, there has been enough to do; and now, all these Schools having burnt or smouldered themselves out, and left nothing but a wide-spread wreck of ashes, dust, and cinders — or perhaps dying embers, kicked to and fro under the feet of innumerable women and children in the magazines, and at best blown here and there into transient sputters, what remains but to adjust ourselves to circumstances? Urge me not," continues this desperate *litterateur*, " with considerations that Poetry, as the inward Voice of Life, must be perennial; only dead in one form to become alive in another; that this still abundant deluge of Metre, seeing there must needs be fractions of Poetry floating, scattered in it, ought still to be net-fished; at all events, surveyed and taken note of. The survey of English metre, at this epoch, perhaps transcends the human faculties; to hire out the reading of it by estimate, at a remunerative rate per page, would, in a few quarters, reduce the cash-box of any extant review to the verge of insolvency."

Such is the humorous but essentially truthful picture of the condition and product of the creative faculties during the second quarter of the present century. The great poets, Byron, Shelley, Wordsworth, Goethe, and Schiller, had fulfilled their tasks and gone to other spheres; and all that remained, with few exceptions, were weak and feeble echoes of their dying strains, caught up and repeated by numerous imitators and pretenders. And so has it ever been; the visions and perceptions of one man become the creed and superficial life-element of other minds. Swedenborg is worthy to be enrolled among the master minds of the world, because he entered for himself into the Arcana of the profoundest mysteries that can concern human intelligences; his great thoughts are revolved, quoted, and represented in all "New Church" publications, but very rarely digested and assimilated by those who claim to be his followers. Still more rare is it to find any receiver of "the heavenly doctrines" determined to enter for himself into the very interiors of all that Swedenborg taught — to see, not the mighty reflections that Swedenborg was able to give of interior realities, but their originals as they stand constellated in the heavens!

But Divine Providence, leading forth the race, as a father the tottering steps of his children, causes the outward form, on which all men are prone to rely, to be forever changing and passing away before their eyes. The seeds of death are ever found lurking in the fairest external appearances, till those externals become the mere correspondences and representatives of interior realities, and then, though enduring as the fadeless garments of the blest, they are ever-varying, as those robes of light change with each changing state. The Coming Age will recognize the profoundest truths in the internal thought of the Swedish sage, while his most tenacious adherents will be forced to admit that, in externals, he often erred, and was not unfrequently deceived. But the discovered error will not only wean them from a blind and bigoted reliance upon frail man, but confirm the sincere lovers of truth in loyalty to her standard. So, also, the Spiritualists are being taught a severe but salutary lesson, that if they will penetrate into the heavenly Arcana of the Inner Life, they must do so by purifying and elevating their own minds, and not by " sitting in circles " or ransacking town and country to find the most " reliable Mediums." Still no step in human progress and development is in vain ; even the falls of the child are essential to its discipline. The mistakes and errors of men are needful while in their present imperfect state. They are to the seekers of truth what trials and losses are to those in the pursuit of wealth ; they but enhance the value of the prize, and confirm the devotion of the true aspirant, as frowns rekindle the ardor of lovers.

Moreover, as man must ever enter into the kingdom of a new unfolding truth with the simplicity and teachableness of little children, it is well that the outer form of the old disappear, that the new may stand alone in its place. It seems also to be a Law that when a change entire and universal is to be outwrought, the means preparatory to its introduction shall be equally widespread, and ultimated to the lowest possible plane. Hence the Spiritual manifestations meet the most external minds ; and allow even the unregenerate to know by experience the fact and process of Spiritual inspiration ; so that scepticism becomes impossible to the candid and living mind. The second step will be, after such have been convinced that Spiritual intercourse is possible, that they learn that it is worse than useless for the purpose of attaining anything desirable, beyond this conviction — except so far as is orderly and directed, not by the will of man, but of God. But as the old form of poetic inspiration died out with Byron and Shelley, Wordsworth and Goethe, and as the miscellaneous Spirit-intercourse itself also as quickly passes away, there will, we apprehend, spring up forms of mediatorial inspiration, of which there will be two permanent types. The first and highest, as it seems to us, will be the opening of the interiors to direct influx to the inspiring sources of love and wisdom. The heavens will flow down into the hearts and lives, into the thought and speech of harmonic natures, as the silent dews impregnate the patient earth. Men will live in heaven, hence they must be inspired by that breath of life that fills its ethereal expanse. A second class of Media will be used for the ultimation, for ends of use and in accordance with Laws of Order, of the creative thoughts and hymns, the Epics and Lyrics, of individual Spirits and societies of Spirits. These will be to the former Media as the youthful artist who copies the work of a-master, to the Angelos and Raphaels, who both design and execute their plans, though they themselves, in their deepest interiors, are instructed and sustained from above.

But in the transition period in which we now are, many varieties of Mediumship must be expected. There are those who stand in rapport with the diseased mentalities of the past and present, and pour forth as Divine Revelations the froth and scum of a receding age; they are the sponges who absorb the waste and impurities of humanity. They are also like running sores that gather the corrupt humors and drain the body of its most noxious fluids. There are others who come in contact with the outmost portion of the Spirit-life. These give crude, and in themselves, false notions of the state of man after death; yet they prepare the way for more truthful disclosures; if in no other way by stimulating the appetite for more substantial nourishment. There are those also who are lifted by genial inspirations to receive influxes from the upper mind-sphere of the age. They stand, as it were, on clear mountains of intellectual elevation, and with keenest perception discern the purer forms of new unfolding truths ere they become sufficiently embodied to be manifest to the grosser minds of the race. Of these Ralph Waldo Emerson is the highest type. He sees the future of truths as our Spirit-seers discern the future of man; he welcomes those impalpable forms, as Spiritualists receive with gladdened minds the returning hosts of Spirit-friends.

There are other mediatorial natures who are in mental and heart-sympathy with man, as he now is, struggling to free himself from the tyranny of the old and effete, and to grasp and retain the new life flowing down from the heavens. And as the kindling rays at first produce more smoke than fire, so their lay is one of promise rather than performance. Such we conceive to be the interior condition of the author of "LEAVES OF GRASS." He accepts man as he is as to his whole nature, and all men as his own brothers. The lambent flame of his genius .encircles the world — nor does he clearly discern between that which is to be preserved, and that which is but as fuel for the purification of the ore from its dross. There is a wild strength, a Spartan simplicity about the man, and he stalks among the dapper gentlemen of this generation, like a drunken Hercules amid the dainty dancers. That his song is highly mediatorial, he himself asserts, though probably he is unacquainted with the Spiritual developments of the age.

" Through me," he sings, "many long dumb voices,
Voices of the interminable generations of slaves,
Voices of the diseased and despairing,
Voices of the cycles of preparation and accretion,
And of threads that connect the stars,
And of the rights of them the others are down upon.

> Through me forbidden voices — voices veiled,
> Voices indecent, by me clarified and transfigured."

We omit much even in this short extract, for the book abounds in passages that cannot be quoted in drawing-rooms, and expressions that fall upon the tympanums of ears polite, with a terrible dissonance. His very gait, as he walks through the world, makes dainty people nervous; and conservatives regard him as a social revolution. His style is everywhere graphic and strong, and he sings many things before untouched in prose or rhyme, in an idiom that is neither prose nor rhyme, nor yet orthodox blank verse. But it serves his purpose well. He wears his strange garb, cut and made by himself, as gracefully as a South American cavalier his poncho. We will continue our quotations.

(Extract of several pages.)

Such are the graphic pictures which this new world-painter flings from his easel and dashes upon the moving panorama of life. His night-thoughts are not less striking, as, borne by the Muse, he looks into every chamber, and hears the quiet breathing of slumbering humanity.

As the volume advances toward its conclusion, the Spirit of the poet becomes calmer and more serenely elevated. But everywhere his sympathy is with *man*, and not with conventionalisms.

.   .   .   .   .   .

We cannot take leave of this remarkable volume without advising our friends who are not too delicately nerved, to study the work as a sign of the times, written, as we perceive, under powerful influxes; a prophecy and promise of much that awaits all who are entering with us into the opening doors of a new era. A portion of that thought which broods over the American nation, is here seized and bodied forth by a son of the people, rudely, wildly, and with some perversions, yet strongly and genuinely, according to the perception of this bold writer. He is the young Hercules who has seized the serpents that would make him and us their prey; but instead of strangling, he would change them to winged and beautiful forms, who shall become the servants of mankind.

———

From Putnam's Monthly, September, 1855.

WALT WHITMAN'S LEAVES OF GRASS. — Our account of the last month's literature would be incomplete without some notice of a curious and lawless collection of poems, called " LEAVES OF GRASS," and issued in a thin quarto, without the name of publisher or author. The poems, twelve in number, are neither in rhyme nor blank verse, but in a sort of excited prose, broken into lines without any attempt at measure or regularity, and, as many readers will perhaps think, without any idea of sense or reason. The writer's scorn for the wonted usages of good writing, extends to the vocabulary he adopts; words usually banished from polite society are here employed without reserve, and with perfect indifference as to their effect on the reader's mind; and not only is the book one not to be read aloud to a mixed audience, but the introduction of terms never before heard or seen, and of slang expressions, often renders an otherwise striking passage altogether laughable. But, as the writer is a new light in poetry, it is only fair to let him state his theory for himself. We extract from the preface:

(Extract.)

The application of these principles, and of many others equally peculiar, which are expounded in a style equally oracular throughout the long preface — is made *passim*, and often with comical success in the poems themselves, which may briefly be described as a compound of the New England transcendentalist and New York rowdy. A fireman or omnibus driver, who had intelligence enough to absorb the speculations of that school of thought which culminated at Boston some fifteen or eighteen years ago, and resources of expression to put them forth again in a form of his own, with sufficient self-conceit and contempt for public taste to affront all usual propriety of diction, might have written this gross yet elevated, this superficial yet profound, this preposterous yet somehow fascinating book. As we say, it is a mixture of Yankee transcendentalism, and New York rowdyism, and, what must be surprising to both these elements, they here seem to fuse and combine with the most perfect harmony. The vast and vague conceptions of the one, lose nothing of their quality in passing through the coarse and odd intellectual medium of the other; while there is an original perception of nature, a manly brawn, and an epic directness in our new poet, which belong to no other adept of the transcendental school. But we have no intention of regularly criticising this very irregular production; our aim is rather to cull, from the rough and ragged thicket of its pages, a few passages equally remarkable in point of thought and expression. Of course we do not select those which are the most transcendental or the most bold.

(Extracts.)

As seems very proper in a book of transcendental poetry, the author withholds his name from the title-page, and presents his portrait, neatly engraved on steel, instead. This, no doubt, is upon the principle that the name is merely accidental; while the portrait affords an idea of the essential being from whom these utterances proceed. We must add, however, that this significant reticence does not prevail throughout the volume, for we learn on p. 29, that our poet is "Walt Whitman, an American, one of the roughs, a kosmos." That he was an American, we knew before, for, aside from America, there is no quarter of the universe where such a production could have had a genesis. That he was one of the roughs was also tolerably plain; but that he was a kosmos, is a piece of news we were hardly prepared for. Precisely what a kosmos is, we hope Walt Whitman will take early occasion to inform the impatient public.

From the American Phrenological Journal, (1856.)

AN ENGLISH AND AN AMERICAN POET.

LEAVES OF GRASS. Poems by Walt Whitman. Brooklyn, 1855. MAUD, and other Poems. By Alfred Tennyson. London, 1855.

It is always reserved for second-rate poems immediately to gratify. As first-rate or natural objects, in their perfect simplicity and proportion, do not startle or strike, but appear no more than matters of course, so probably natural poetry does not, for all its being the rarest, and telling of the longest and largest work. The artist or writer whose talent is to please the connoisseurs of his time, may obey the laws of his time, and achieve the intense and elaborated beauty of parts. The perfect poet cannot afford any special beauty of parts, or to limit himself by any laws less than those universal ones of the great masters, which include all times, and all men and women, and the living and the dead. For from the study of the universe is drawn this irrefragable truth, that the law of the requisites of a grand poem, or any other complete workmanship, is originality, and the average and superb beauty of the ensemble. Possessed with this law, the fitness of aim, time, persons, places, surely follows. Possessed with this law, and doing justice to it, no poet or any one else will make anything ungraceful or mean, any more than any emanation of nature is.

The poetry of England, by the many rich geniuses of that wonderful little island, has grown out of the facts of the English race, the monarchy and aristocracy prominent over the rest, and conforms to the spirit of them. No nation ever did or ever will receive with national affection any poets except those born of its national blood. Of these, the writings express the finest infusions of government, traditions, faith, and the dependence or independence of a people, and even the good or bad physiognomy, and the ample or small geography. Thus what very properly fits a subject of the British crown may fit very ill an American freeman. No fine romance, no inimitable delineation of character, no grace of delicate illustrations, no rare picture of shore or mountain or sky, no deep thought of the intellect, is so important to a man as his opinion of himself is; everything receives its tinge from that. In the verse of all those undoubtedly great writers, Shakspeare just as much as the rest, there is the air which to America is the air of death. The mass of the people, the laborers and all who serve, are slag, refuse. The countenances of kings and great lords are beautiful; the countenances of mechanics are ridiculous and deformed. What play of Shakspeare, represented in America, is not an insult to America, to the marrow in its bones? How can the tone never silent in their plots and characters be applauded, unless Washington should have been caught and hung, and Jefferson was the most enormous of liars, and common persons, north and south, should bow low to their betters, and to organic superiority of blood? Sure as the heavens envelop the earth, if the Americans want a race of bards worthy of 1855, and of the stern reality of this republic, they must cast around for men essentially different from the old poets, and from the modern successions of jinglers and snivellers and fops.

English versification is full of these danglers, and America follows after them. Every body writes poetry, and yet there is not a single poet. An age greater than the proudest of the past is swiftly slipping away, without one lyric voice to seize its greatness, and speak it as an encouragement and onward lesson. We have heard, by many grand announcements, that he was to come, but will he come?

> A mighty Poet whom this age shall choose
> To be its spokesman to all coming times.
> In the ripe full-blown season of his soul,
> He shall go forward in his spirit's strength,
> And grapple with the questions of all time,
> And wring from them their meanings. As King Saul
> Called up the buried prophet from his grave
> To speak his doom, so shall this Poet-king
> Call up the dread past from its awful grave
> To tell him of our future. As the air
> Doth sphere the world, so shall his heart of love—
> Loving mankind, not peoples. As the lake
> Reflects the flower, tree, rock, and bending heaven,
> Shall he reflect our great humanity;
> And as the young Spring breathes with living breath
> On a dead branch, till it sprouts fragrantly
> Green leaves and sunny flowers, shall he breathe life
> Through every theme he touch, making all Beauty
> And Poetry forever like the stars.   (*Alexander Smith.*)

The best of the school of poets at present received in Great Britain and America is Alfred Tennyson. He is the bard of ennui and of the aristocracy, and their combination into love. This love is the old stock love of playwrights and romancers, Shakspeare the same as the rest. It is possessed of the same unnatural and shocking passion for some girl or woman, that wrenches it from its manhood, emasculated and impotent, without strength to hold the rest of the objects and goods of life in their proper positions. It seeks nature for sickly uses. It goes screaming and weeping after the facts of the universe, in their calm beauty and equanimity, to note the occurrence of itself, and to sound the news, in connection with the charms of the neck, hair, or complexion of a particular female.

Poetry, to Tennyson and his British and American eleves, is a gentleman of the first degree, boating, fishing, and shooting genteelly through nature, admiring the ladies, and talking to them, in company, with that elaborate half-choked deference that is to be made up by the terrible license of men among themselves. The spirit of the burnished society of upper-class England fills this writer and his effusions from top to toe. Like that, he does not ignore courage and the superior qualities of men, but all is to show forth through dandified forms. He meets the nobility and gentry half-way. The models are the same both to the poet and the parlors. Both have the same supercilious elegance, both love the reminiscences which extol caste, both agree on the topics proper for mention and discussion, both hold the same undertone of church and state, both have the same languishing melancholy and irony, both indulge largely in persiflage, both are marked by the contour of high blood and a constitutional aversion to anything cowardly and mean, both accept the love depicted in romances as the great business of a life or a poem, both seem unconscious of the mighty truths of eternity and immortality, both are silent on the presumptions of liberty and equality, and both devour themselves in solitary lassitude. Whatever may be said of all this, it harmonizes and represents facts. The present phases of high-life in Great Britain are as natural a growth there, as Tennyson and his poems are a natural growth of those phases. It remains to be distinctly admitted that this man is a real first-class poet, infused amid all that ennui and aristocracy.

Meanwhile a strange voice parts others aside and demands for its owner that position that is only allowed after the seal of many returning years has stamped with approving stamp the claims of the loftiest leading genius. Do you think the best honors of the earth are won so easily, Walt Whitman? Do you think city and country are to fall before the vehement egotism of your recitative of yourself?

I am the poet of the body,
And I am the poet of the soul.

The pleasures of heaven are with me, and the pains of hell are with me,
The first I graft and increase upon myself, the latter I translate into a new tongue.

I am the poet of the woman the same as the man,
And I say it is as great to be a woman as to be a man,
And I say there is nothing greater than the mother of men.

I chant a new chant of dilation or pride,
We have had ducking and deprecating about enough,
I show that size is only development.

It is indeed a strange voice! Critics and lovers and readers of poetry as hitherto written, may well be excused the chilly and unpleasant shudders which will assuredly run through them, to their very blood and bones, when they first read Walt Whitman's poems. If this is poetry, where must its foregoers stand? And what is at once to become of the ranks of rhymesters, melancholy and swallow-tailed, and of all the confectioners and upholsterers of verse, if the tan-faced man here advancing and claiming to speak for America and the nineteenth hundred of the Christian list of years, typifies indeed the natural and proper bard?

The theory and practice of poets have hitherto been to select certain ideas or events or personages, and then describe them in the best manner they could, always with as much ornament as the case allowed. Such are not the theory and practice of the new poet. He never presents for perusal a poem ready-made on the old models, and ending when you come to the end of it; but every sentence and every passage tells of an interior not always seen, and exudes an impalpable something which sticks to him that reads, and pervades and provokes him to tread the half-invisible road where the poet, like an apparition, is striding fearlessly before. If Walt Whitman's premises are true, then there is a subtler range of poetry than that of the grandeur of acts and events, as in Homer, or of characters, as in Shakspeare—poetry to which all other writing is subservient, and which confronts the very meanings of the works of nature and competes with them. It is the direct bringing of occurrences and persons and things to bear on the listener or beholder, to re-appear through him or her; and it offers the best way of making them a part of him and her as the right aim of the greatest poet.

Of the spirit of life in visible forms—of the spirit of the seed growing out of the ground—of the spirit of the resistless motion of the globe passing unsuspected but quick as lightning along its orbit—of them is the spirit of this man's poetry. Like them it eludes and mocks criticism, and appears unerringly in results. Things, facts, events, persons, days, ages, qualities, tumble pell-mell, exhaustless and copious, with what appear to be the same disregard of parts, and the same absence of special purpose, as in nature. But the voice of the few rare and controlling critics, and the voice of more than one generation of men, or two generations of men, must speak for the inexpressible purposes of nature, and for this haughtiest of writers that has ever yet written and printed a book. His is to prove either the most lamentable of failures or the most glorious of triumphs, in the known history of literature. And after all we have written we confess our brain-felt and heart-felt inability to decide which we think it is likely to be.

From the Critic. (London, England.)

LEAVES OF GRASS. New York, 1855. London : Horsell.

We had ceased, we imagined, to be surprised at anything that America could produce. We had become stoically indifferent to her Woolly Horses, her Mermaids, her Sea Serpents, her Barnums, and so forth ;—but the last monstrous importation from Brooklyn, New York, has scattered our indifference to the winds. Here is a thin quarto volume without an author's name on the title-page ; but to atone for which we have a portrait engraved on steel of the notorious individual who is the poet presumptive. This portrait expresses all the features of the hard democrat, and none of the flexile delicacy of the civilized poet. The damaged hat, the rough beard, the naked throat, the shirt exposed to the waist, are each and all presented to show that the man to whom these articles belong scorns the delicate arts of civilization. The man is the true impersonation of his book—rough, uncouth, vulgar. It was by the merest accident that we discovered the name of this erratic and newest wonder; but at page 29 we find that he is —

Walt Whitman, an American, one of the roughs, a kosmos,
Disorderly, fleshly, and sensual.

The words "an American" are a surplusage, "one of the roughs" too painfully apparent; but what is intended to be conveyed by "a kosmos" we cannot tell, unless it means a man who thinks that the fine essence of poetry consists in writing a book which an American reviewer is compelled to declare is "not to be read aloud to a mixed audience." We should have passed over this book, "LEAVES OF GRASS," with indignant contempt, had not some few Transatlantic critics attempted to "fix" this Walt Whitman as the poet who shall give a new and independent literature to America — who shall form a race of poets as Banquo's issue formed a line of kings. Is it possible that the most prudish nation in the world will adopt a poet whose indecencies stink in the nostrils ? We hope not; and yet there is a probability, and we will show why, that this Walt Whitman will not meet with the stern rebuke which he so richly deserves. America has felt, oftener perhaps than we have declared, that she has no national poet — that each one of her children of song has relied too much on European inspiration, and clung too fervently to the old conventionalities. It is therefore not unlikely that she may believe in the dawn of a thoroughly original literature, now there has arisen a man who scorns the Hellenic deities, who has no belief in, perhaps because he has no knowledge of, Homer and Shakspeare ; who relies on his own rugged nature, and trusts to his own rugged language, being himself what he shows in his poems. Once transfix him as the genesis of a new era, and the manner of the man may be forgiven or forgotten. But what claim has this Walt Whitman to be thus considered, or to be considered a poet at all ? We grant freely enough that he has a strong relish for nature and freedom, just as an animal has ; nay, further, that his crude mind is capable of appreciating some of nature's beauties ; but it by no means follows that, because nature is excellent, therefore art is contemptible. Walt Whitman is as unacquainted with art, as a hog is with mathematics. His poems — we must call them so for convenience — twelve in number, are innocent of rhythm, and resemble nothing so much as the war-cry of the Red Indians. Indeed, Walt Whitman has had near and ample opportunities of studying the vociferations of a few amiable savages. Or rather, perhaps, this Walt Whitman reminds us of Caliban flinging down his logs, and setting himself to write a poem. In fact, Caliban, and not Walt Whitman, might have written this :

> I too am not a bit tamed — I too am untranslatable,
> I sound my *barbaric yawp* over the roofs of the world.

Is this man with the " barbaric yawp " to push Longfellow into the shade, and he meanwhile to stand and " make mouths " at the sun ? The chance of this might be formidable were it not ridiculous. That object or that act which most develops the ridiculous element carries in its bosom the seeds of decay, and is wholly powerless to trample out of God's universe one spark of the beautiful. We do not, then, fear this Walt Whitman, who gives us slang in the place of melody, and rowdyism in the place of regularity. The depth of his indecencies will be the grave of his fame, or ought to be if all proper feeling is not extinct. The very nature of this man's compositions excludes us from proving by extracts the truth of our remarks; but we, who are not prudish, emphatically declare that the man who wrote page 79 of the " LEAVES OF GRASS " deserves nothing so richly as the public executioner's whip. Walt Whitman libels the highest type of humanity, and calls his free speech the true utterance of *a man :* we, who may have been misdirected by civilization, call it the expression of *a beast*.

The leading idea of Walt Whitman's poems is as old as the hills. It is the doctrine of universal sympathy which the first poet maintained, and which the last on earth will maintain also. He says :

> "Not a mutineer walks handcuffed to the jail, but I am handcuffed to him and
>   walk by his side.
> Not a cholera patient lies at the last gasp, but I also lie at the last gasp."

To show this sympathy he instances a thousand paltry, frivolous, and obscene circumstances. Herein we may behold the difference between a great and a contemptible poet. What

Shakspeare — mighty shade of the mightiest bard, forgive us the comparison! — expressed in a single line,

"One touch of nature makes the whole world kin,"

this Walt Whitman has tortured into scores of pages. A single extract will show what we mean. This miserable spinner of words declares that the earth has "no themes, or hints, or provokers," and never had, if you cannot find such themes, or hints, or provokers in —

(*Extract.*)

Can it be possible that its author intended this as a portion of a poem? Is it not more reasonable to suppose that Walt Whitman has been learning to write, and that the compositor has got hold of his copy-book? The American critics are, in the main, pleased with this man because he is self-reliant, and because he assumes all the attributes of his country. If Walt Whitman has really assumed those attributes, America should hasten to repudiate them, be they what they may. The critics are pleased also because he talks like a man unaware that there was ever such a production as a book, or ever such a being as a writer. This in the present day is a qualification exceedingly rare, and *may* be valuable, so we wish those gentlemen joy of their GREAT UNTAMED.

We must not neglect to quote an unusual passage, which may be suggestive to writers of the Old World. To silence our incredulous readers, we assure them that the passage may be found at page 92.

(*Extract.*)

The tansformation and the ethereal nature of Walt Whitman is marvellous to us, but perhaps not so to a nation from which the spirit-rappers sprung.   .   -

I depart as air, I shake my white locks at the runaway sun,
I effuse my flesh in eddies, and drift it in lacy jags;
I bequeath myself to the dirt, to grow from the grass I love,
If you want me again, look for me under your boot-soles.

Here is also a sample of the man's slang and vulgarity:

(*Extract.*)

And here a spice of his republican insolence, his rank Yankeedom, and his audacious trifling with death:

Dig out King George's coffin, unwrap him quick from the grave-clothes, box up
    his bones for a journey,
Find a swift Yankee clipper: here is freight for you, black-bellied clipper,
Up with your anchor! shake out your sails! steer straight toward Boston Bay.

The committee open the box and set up the regal ribs, and glue those that will
    not stay,
And clap the skull on top of the ribs, and clap a crown on top of the skull.

We will neither weary nor insult our readers with more extracts from this notable book. Emerson *has praised it*, and called it the "most extraordinary piece of wit and wisdom America has yet contributed." Because Emerson has grasped substantial fame, he can afford to be generous, but Emerson's generosity must not be mistaken for justice. If this work is really a work of genius — if the principles of those poems, their free language, their amazing and audacious egotism, their animal vigor, be real poetry and the divinest evidence of the true poet — then our studies have been in vain, and vainer still the homage which we have paid the monarchs of Saxon intellect — Shakspeare, and Milton, and Byron. This Walt Whitman holds that his claim to be a poet lies in his robust and rude health. He is, in fact, as he declares, "the poet of the body." Adopt this theory, and Walt Whitman is a Titan; Shelley and Keats the merest pigmies. If we had commenced a notice of "LEAVES OF GRASS" in anger, we could not but dismiss it in grief, for its author, we have just discovered, is conscious of his affliction. He says, at page 33,

I am given up by traitors;
I talk wildly, I am mad.

From the Examiner. (London, England, 1857.)

LEAVES OF GRASS. Brooklyn, New York.

We have too long overlooked in this country the great poet who has recently arisen in America, of whom some of his countrymen speak in connection with Bacon and Shakspeare; whom others compare with Tennyson — much to the disadvantage of our excellent laureate — and to whom Mr. Emerson writes that he finds in his book "incomparable things, said incomparably well." The book he pronounces "the most extraordinary piece of wit and wisdom that America has yet contributed;" at which, indeed, says Mr. Emerson in the printed letter sent to us — "I rubbed my eyes a little, to see if this sunbeam were no illusion."

No illusion truly is Walt Whitman, the new American prodigy, who, as he is himself candid enough to intimate, sounds his barbaric yawp over the roofs of the world. He is described by one of his own local papers as "a tenderly affectionate, rowdyish, contemplative, sensual, moral, susceptible, and imperious person," who aspires to cast some of his own grit, whatever that may be, into literature. We have ourselves been disposed to think there is in literature grit enough, according to the ordinary sense, but decidedly Walt Whitman tosses in some more. The author describes himself as "one of the roughs, a kosmos;" indeed, he seems to be very much impressed with the fact that he is a kosmos, and repeats it frequently. A kosmos we may define, from the portrait of it on the front of the book, is a gentleman in his shirt-sleeves, with one hand in a pocket of his pantaloons, and his wide-awake cocked with a damme-sir air over his forehead.

On the other hand, according to an American review that flatters Walt Whitman, this kosmos is a " compound of the New England transcendentalist and New York rowdy."

But as such terms of compliment may not be quite clear to English readers, we must be content, in simpler fashion, to describe to them this Brooklyn boy as a wild Tupper of the West. We can describe him perfectly by a few suppositions. Suppose that Mr. Tupper had been brought up to the business of an auctioneer, then banished to the backwoods, compelled to live for a long time as a backwoodsman, and thus contracting a passion for the reading of Emerson and Carlyle; suppose him maddened by this course of reading, and fancying himself not only an Emerson but a Carlyle and an American Shakspeare to boot, when the fits come on, and putting forth his notion of that combination in his own self-satisfied way, and in his own wonderful cadences? In that state he would write a book exactly like Walt Whitman's "LEAVES OF GRASS."

(Extracts and Interlineated remarks.)

We must be just to Walt Whitman in allowing that he has one positive merit. His verse has a purpose. He desires to assert the pleasure that a man has in himself, his body and its sympathies, his mind (in a lesser degree, however) and its sympathies. He asserts man's right to express his delight in animal enjoyment, and the harmony in which he should stand, body and soul, with fellow-men and the whole universe. To express this, and to declare that the poet is the highest manifestation of this, generally also to suppress shams, is the purport of these "LEAVES OF GRASS." Perhaps it might have been done as well, however, without being always so purposely obscene, and intentionally foul-mouthed, as Walt Whitman is.

(Extracts and Interlineations.)

In the construction of our artificial Whitman, we began with the requirement that a certain philosopher should have been bred to the business of an auctioneer. We must add now, to complete the imitation of Walt Whitman, that the wild philosopher and poet, as conceived by us, should be perpetually haunted by the delusion that he has a catalogue to make. Threefourths of Walt Whitman's book is poetry as catalogues of auctioneers are poems. Whenever any general term is used, off the mind wanders on this fatal track, and an attempt is made to specify all lots included under it. Does Walt Whitman speak of a town, he is at once ready with pages of town lots. Does he mention the American country, he feels bound thereupon to draw up a list of barns, wagons, wilds, mountains, animals, trees, people, "a Hoosier, a Badger, a Buckeye, a Louisianian or Georgian, a poke-easy from sand-hills and pines," &c., &c. We will give an illustration of this form of lunacy. The subject from which the patient starts off is equivalent to things in general, and we can spare room only for half the catalogue. It will be enough, however, to show how there arises catalogue within catalogue, and how sorely the paroxysm is aggravated by the incidental mention of any one particular that is itself again capable of subdivision into lots.

The usual routine, the workshop, factory, yard. office, store, or desk;
The jaunt of hunting or fishing, or the life of hunting or fishing,
Pasture-life, foddering, milking and herding, and all the personnel and usages;
The plum-orchard and apple-orchard, gardening, seedlings, cuttings, flowers and vines,
Grains and manures, marl, clay, loam, the subsoil plough, the shovel and pick and rake and hoe, irrigation and draining;
The currycomb, the horse-cloth, the halter and bridle and bits, the very wisps of straw,
The barn and barn-yard, the bins and mangers, the mows and racks;
Manufactures, commerce, engineering, the building of cities, and every trade carried on there, and the implements of every trade.

(Extract continued.)

Now let us compare with this a real auctioneer's catalogue. We will take that of Goldsmith's chambers, by way of departing as little as we can from the poetical. For, as Walt Whitman would say (and here we quote quite literally, prefixing only a verse of our own, from "A Catalogue of the Household Furniture with the select collection of scarce, curious, and valuable books of Dr. Goldsmith, deceased, which by order of the admʳ, will be sold by auction," &c., &c.)

(The Examiner's burlesque of Walt Whitman.)

Surely the house of a poet is a poem, and behold a poet in the auctioneer who tells you the whole lot of it —
The bath stone, compass front, open border, fender, shovel, tongs, and poker,
The blue moreen festoon window-curtain, the mahogany dining-table on the floor,
The six ditto hollow seat chairs covered with blue moreen,
Covered with blue moreen and finished with a double row of brass nails and check cases,
The Wilton carpet, sun shade, line and pulleys, the deal sideboard stained,
The teapot, five coffee cups, sugar basin and cover, four saucers and six cups,
Two quart decanters and stoppers, one plain ditto, eleven glasses, one wine and water glass,
A pair of bellows and a brush, a footman, copper tea-kettle and coal-scuttle.
Two pairs of plated candlesticks,
A mahogany teaboard, a pet bordered ditto, a large round japanned ditto and two waiters.
The Tragic Muse in a gold frame.

After all, we are not sure whether the poetry of that excellent Mr. Good, the auctioneer who, at his Great Room, No. 121 Fleet Street, sold the household furniture of Oliver Goldsmith in the summer of 1774, does not transcend in wisdom and in wit, 'the most extraordinary piece of wit and wisdom that" (according to Mr. Emerson) "America has yet contributed."

From the London Leader. (1857.)

TRANSATLANTIC LATTER–DAY POETRY.

LEAVES OF GRASS. Brooklyn, New York, 1855. London: Horsell.

"Latter-day poetry" in America is of a very different character from the same manifestation in the old country. Here it is occupied for the most part with dreams of the middle ages, of the old knightly and religious times; in America it is employed chiefly with the present, except when it travels out into the undiscovered future. Here our latter-day poets are apt to whine over the times, as if heaven were perpetually betraying the earth with a show of progress that is in fact retrogression, like the backward advance of crabs; there, the minstrels of the stars and stripes blow a loud note of exultation before the grand new epoch, and think the Greeks and Romans, the early Oriental races, and the later men of the middle centuries, of small account before the onward tramping of these present generations. Of this latter sect is a certain phenomenon who has recently started up in Brooklyn, New York — one Walt Whitman, author of "LEAVES OF GRASS," who has been received by a section of his countrymen as a sort of prophet, and by Englishmen as a kind of fool. For ourselves, we are not disposed to accept him as the one, having less faith in latter-day prophets than in latter-day poets; but assuredly we cannot regard him as the other. Walt is one of the most amazing, one of the most startling, one of the most perplexing creations of the modern American mind; but he is no fool, though abundantly eccentric, nor is his book mere food for laughter, though undoubtedly containing much that may easily and fairly be turned into ridicule.

The singularity of the author's mind — his utter disregard of ordinary forms and modes — appears in the very title-page and frontispiece of his work. Not only is there no author's name, (which in itself would not be singular,) but there is no publisher's name — that of the English bookseller being a London addition. Fronting the title is a portrait of a bearded gentleman in his shirt-sleeves and a Spanish hat, with an all-pervading atmosphere of Yankee-doodle about him; but again there is no patronymic, and we can only infer that this roystering blade is the author of the book. Then follows a long prose treatise by way of preface (and here once more the anonymous system is carried out, the treatise having no heading whatever;) and after that we have the poem, in the course of which a short autobiographical discourse reveals to us the name of the author.

(*Extract from Preface.*)

The poem is written in wild, irregular, unrhymed, almost

unmetrical "lengths," like the measured prose of Mr. Martin
Farquhar Tupper's *Proverbial Philosophy*, or some of the Oriental writings. The external form, therefore, is startling, and
by no means seductive to English ears, accustomed to the
sumptuous music of ordinary metre; and the central principle
of the poem is equally staggering. It seems to resolve itself
into an all-attracting egotism — an eternal presence of the individual soul of Walt Whitman in all things, yet in such wise
that this one soul shall be presented as a type of all human
souls whatsoever. He goes forth into the world, this rough,
devil-may-care Yankee; passionately identifies himself with all
forms of being, sentient or inanimate; sympathizes deeply with
humanity; riots with a kind of Bacchanal fury in the force and
fervor of his own sensations; will not have the most vicious or
abandoned shut out from final comfort and reconciliation; is
delighted with Broadway, New York, and equally in love with
the desolate backwoods, and the long stretch of the uninhabit-
ed prairie, where the wild beasts wallow in the reeds, and the
wilder birds start upward from their nests among the grass;
perceives a divine mystery wherever his feet conduct, or his
thoughts transport him; and beholds all things tending toward
the central and sovereign Me. Such, as we conceive, is the key
to this strange, grotesque, and bewildering book; yet we are
far from saying that the key will unlock all the quirks and oddities of the volume. Much remains of which we confess we can
make nothing; much that seems to us purely fantastical and
preposterous; much that appears to our muddy vision gratui-
tously prosaic, needlessly plain-speaking, disgusting without
purpose, and singular without result. There are so many evi-
dences of a noble soul in Whitman's pages that we regret these
aberrations, which only have the effect of discrediting what is
genuine by the show of something false; and especially do we
deplore the unnecessary openness with which Walt reveals to
us matters which ought rather to remain in sacred silence. It
is good not to be ashamed of Nature; it is good to have an all-
inclusive charity; but it is also good, sometimes, to leave the
veil across the Temple.

———

From the Brooklyn Daily Times. (1856.)

LEAVES OF GRASS, — Brooklyn, N. Y. — 1856.

This is a new, enlarged and stereotyped, edition of that singular production of "Walt Whitman," whose first appearance,
in 1855, created such an extraordinary sensation in the literary
world on both sides of the Atlantic. The first edition — which
was duly noticed in these columns — contained twelve poems.
In the present edition those poems are revised, and twenty

others are added. The form of the book has been changed
from 4to. to 16mo., and the typography is much improved.

The work, in its singular character, we understand to be an
assertion of a two-fold individuality for the author: of himself
personally, and of himself nationally; and the author, by example at least, to be an advocate of as much for all of his nation.
A bold example he sets. The titles of the poems are various,
and the poems under them present differences; yet through
them all, with whatever else, runs one vital view; one ontologi-
cal lesson in the same idiosyncratic strain.

Fanciful, fertile, and free in words, yet often, conventionally
speaking, inelegant, and sometimes downright low; simple, ab
rupt, and detached sentences; frequently aphoristic, yet diffuse
and uniform, sometimes to tediousness; at times strikingly
clear and forcible, and again impenetrably obscure; a meeting
of the extremes of literalness and meteleptic figures — of tire-
some superficial details and comprehensive subtle generalities,
oddities, ruggedness and strength; these are the chief characteristics of his style. There occur frequent instances of all-
important and majestic thought, and so fitly expressed that the
dissonance to the unaccustomed ears of the reader cannot pre-
vent his stopping to admire. The matter is characterized by
thought rather than by sentiment. The right and duty of man
with the passions are enjoined and celebrated, rather than the
passions themselves. There are speculative philosophies ad-
vanced, upon which readers will differ with the author and with
each other; and some of these to intolerant conventionalists
will give offence. We are not prepared to indorse them all ourselves. And there are practical philosophies of which he treats,
destined to encounter fiercer repugnance. But the book is not
one that warrants its dismissal with disgust or contempt. There
is a deep substratum of observant and contemplative wisdom, as
broad as the foundation of society, running through it all; and
whatever else there is of questionable good, so much at-least is
a genuine pearl that we cannot afford to trample under our feet.
The poems contain some lessons of the highest importance,
and possess a further value in their strong suggestiveness. We
accord to the leading idea of the work alone, personal and national individuality, exemplified and recommended as it is, an
incalculable value. The poems improve upon a second reading,
and they may commonly require a repetition in order to a de-
served appreciation, like a strange piece of music with subtle
harmonies.

The work is altogether *sui generis*, unless we call it Emer-
sonian. That name is ample enough to cover a multitude of
oddities and excellences; but that it is not shaped to all the
radiations of the unbridled muse of the author under notice we
think a single extract from his first poem will show.

(*Extracts.*)

From the Monthly Trade Gazette. (*New York*, 1856.)

LEAVES OF GRASS. By Walt Whitman. A poem that deserves and will eventually obtain a higher niche in Fame's temple, than all the "———s" ever written. There is a sturdy strength — a far-reaching grasp of Titanic thought, boldly, manfully, and appositely expressed — and a fillibuster-like daring running, like a strong, vigorous river, through its diction, which impress the reader with the conviction that he is in the presence of a more than ordinary man. The poem is written without regard to metrical rules, which the author evidently looks upon as puerile — in which we think he is nearer right than wrong — but it bears in every line the stamp of rude but sterling genius. The mean manner in which it is put forth by its publishers, however, will seriously interfere with its chances of publicity. Had it been issued in a dress worthy of the matter, it could hardly fail of mounting, at a single step, to the topmost floor of Novelty's platform, and instantly commanding the public eye. As it is, its success will be a work of time. We give a cordial greeting to *Leaves of Grass*, which we look upon as the most considerable poem that has yet appeared in our country.

———

From " Fourteen Thousand Miles Afoot." (*N. Y.*, 1859.)

Nothing can more clearly demonstrate the innate vulgarity of our American people, their radical immodesty, their internal licentiousness, their unchastity of heart, their foulness of feeling, than the tabooing of Walt Whitman's "Leaves of Grass." It is quite impossible to find a publisher for the new edition which has long since been ready for the press, so measureless is the depravity of public taste. There is not an indecent word, an immodest expression, in the entire volume; not a suggestion which is not purity itself; and yet it is rejected on account of its indecency ! So much do I think of this work by the healthiest and most original poet America has produced, so valuable a means is it of rightly estimating character, that I have been accustomed to try with it of what quality was the virtue my friends possessed. How few stood the test I shall not say. Some did, and praised it beyond measure. These I set down without hesitation as radically pure, as "born again," and fitted for the society of heaven and the angels. And this test I would recommend to every one. Would you, reader, male or female, ascertain if you be actually modest, innocent, pure-minded? read the "Leaves of Grass." If you find nothing improper there, you are one of the virtuous and pure. If, on the contrary, you find your sense of decency shocked, then is that sense of decency an exceedingly foul one, and you, man or woman, a very vulgar, dirty person.

The atmosphere of the " Leaves of Grass " is as sweet as that of a hay-field. Its pages exhale the fragrance of nature. It takes you back to man's pristine state of innocence in Paradise, and lifts you Godwards. It is the healthiest book, morally, this century has produced; and if it were reprinted in the form of a cheap tract, and scattered broadcast over the land, put into the hands of youth, and into the hands of men and women everywhere, it would do more towards elevating our nature, towards eradicating this foul, vulgar, licentious, sham modesty, which so degrades our people now, than any other means within my knowledge. What we want is not outward, but inward modesty, not external, but internal virtue, not silk and broadcloth decency, but a decency infused into every organ of the body and faculty of the soul. Is modesty a virtue ? Is it then worn in clothes ? Does it hang over the shoulders, or does it live and breathe in the heart ? Our modesty is a Jewish phylactery, sewed up in the padding of a coat, and stitched into a woman's stays.

From the Brooklyn Daily Eagle. (1856.)

"LEAVES OF GRASS,"—AN EXTRAORDINARY BOOK.

Here we have a book which fairly staggers us. It sets all the ordinary rules of criticism at defiance. It is one of the strangest compounds of transcendentalism, bombast, philosophy, folly, wisdom, wit, and dulness which it ever entered into the heart of man to conceive. Its author is Walt Whitman, and the book is a reproduction of the author. His name is not on the frontispiece, but his portrait, half length, is. The contents of the book form a daguerreotype of his inner being, and the title page bears a representation of its physical tabernacle.- It is a poem ; but it conforms to none of the rules by which poetry has ever been judged. It is not an epic, nor an ode, nor a lyric ; nor does its verse move with the measured pace of poetical feet — of iambic, trochaic, or anapestic, nor seek the aid of amphibrach, of dactyl, or spondee, nor of final or cesural pause, except by accident. But we had better give Walt's own conception of what a poet of the age and country should be. We quote from the preface :

" His spirit responds to his country's spirit; he incarnates its geography and natural life, and rivers and lakes. Mississippi with annual freshets and changing chutes — Missouri, and Columbia, and Ohio, and the beautiful masculine Hudson, do not embouchure where they spend themselves more than they embouchure into him. The blue breadth over the inland sea of Virginia and Maryland, and the sea off Massachusetts and Maine, and over Manhattan Bay, over Champlain and Erie, and over Ontario and Huron, and Michigan and Superior, and over the Texan, and Mexican, and Floridian, and Cuban seas, and over the seas off California and Oregon — is not tallied by the blue breadth of the waters below, more than the breadth of above and below is tallied by him."
* * * " To him enter the essence of the real things, and past and present

events—of the enormous diversity of temperature, and agriculture, and mines—
the tribes of red aborigines—the weather-beaten vessels entering new ports or
making landings on rocky coasts—the first settlement North and South—the
rapid stature and muscle—the haughty defiance of '76, and the war, and peace,
and formation of the constitution—the Union always surrounded by blusther-
ers, and always calm and impregnable—the immigrants—the wharf-hemmed
cities and superior marine—the unsurveyed interior—the log houses, and clearings, and wild animals, and hunters, and trappers—the free commerce, the fishing, and whaling, and gold digging—the endless gestation of new States—the
convening of Congress every December, the members duly coming up from all climates and the uttermost parts—the noble character of the young mechanics, and
of all free American workmen and workwomen—the general ardor, and friend-
liness, and enterprise—the perfect equality of the female with the male—the
large amativeness—the fluid movement of the population," &c. * * * "For
such the expression of the American poet is to be transcendent and new."

And the poem seems to accord with the ideas here laid down.
No drawing-room poet is the author of the "Leaves of Grass;"
he prates not of guitar-thrumming under ladies' windows, nor
deals in the extravagances of sentimentalism; no pretty conceits or polished fancies are tacked together "like orient pearls
at random strung;" but we have the free utterance of an un-
trammelled spirit without the slightest regard to established
models or fixed standards of taste. His scenery presents no
shaven lawns or neatly trimmed arbors; no hothouse conser-
vatory, where delicate exotics odorize the air and enchant the
eye. If we follow the poet we must scale unknown precipices
and climb untrodden mountains; or we boat on nameless lakes,
encountering probably rapids and waterfalls, and start wild
fowls never classified by Wilson or Audubon; or we wander
among primeval forests, now pressing the yielding surface of
velvet moss, and anon caught among thickets and brambles.
He believes in the ancient philosophy that there is no more
real beauty or merit in one particle of matter than another; he
appreciates all; everything is right that is in its place, and
everything is wrong that is not in its place. He is guilty, not
only of breaches of conventional decorum, but treats with nonchalant defiance what goes by the name of refinement and delicacy of feeling and expression. Whatever is natural he takes
to his heart; whatever is artificial—in the frivolous sense—he
makes of no account. The following description of himself is
more truthful than many self-drawn pictures:

"Apart from the pulling and hauling, stands what I am,
Stands amused, complacent, compassionate, idle, unitary,
Looks down, is erect, bends an arm on an impalpable certain rest,
Looks with its side-curved head, curious what will come next,
Both in and out of the game, and watching and wondering at it."

As a poetic interpretation of nature, we believe the following
is not surpassed in the range of poetry:

"A child said, What is the grass? fetching it to me with full hands;
How could I answer the child? I do not know any more than he.

I guess it is the handkerchief of the Lord,
A scented gift and remembrancer designedly dropped,
Bearing the owner's name someway in the corners, that we may see and remark,
  and say, Whose?"

We are afforded glimpses of half-formed pictures to tease
and tantalize with their indistinctness; like a crimson cheek
and flashing eye looking on us through the leaves of an arbor
—mocking us for a moment, but vanishing before we can reach
them.   Here is an example:

> "Twenty-eight young men bathe by the shore,
> Twenty-eight young men and all so friendly;
> Twenty-eight years of womanly life and all so lonesome.
>
> She owns the fine house by the rise of the bank;
> She hides handsome and richly drest aft the blinds of the window.
>
> Which of the young men does she like the best?
> Ah, the homeliest of them is beautiful to her.
>
> Dancing and laughing along the beach came the twenty-ninth bather;
> The rest did not see her, but she saw them," &c.

Well, did the lady fall in love with the twenty-ninth bather,
or *vice versa?*   Our author scorns to gratify such puerile curiosity; the denouement which novel readers would expect is not
hinted at.

In his philosophy justice attains its proper dimensions:

> "I play not a march for victors only: I play great marches for conquered and
>   slain persons.
>
> Have you heard that it was good to gain the day?
> I also say that it is good to fall—battles are lost in the same spirit in which they
>   are won;
> I sound triumphal drums for the dead—I fling thro' my embouchures the
>   loudest and gayest music for them.
>
> Vivas to those who have failed and to those whose war vessels sank in the sea,
> And to those themselves who sank into the sea,
> And to all generals that lost engagements, and all overcome heroes, and the
>   numberless unknown heroes, equal to the greatest heroes known."

The triumphs of victors had been duly celebrated, but surely
a poet was needed to sing the praises of the defeated whose
cause was righteous, and the heroes who had been trampled
under the hoofs of iniquity's onward march.

He does not pick and choose sentiments and expressions fit
for general circulation—he gives a voice to whatever *is*, whatever we see, and hear, and think, and feel.   He descends to
grossness, which debars the poem from being read aloud in any
mixed circle.   We have said that the work defies criticism; we
pronounce no judgment upon it; it is a work that will satisfy
few upon a first perusal; it must be read again and again, and
then it will be to many unaccountable.   All who read it will
agree that it is an extraordinary book, full of beauties and
blemishes, such as Nature is to those who have only a half-
formed acquaintance with her mysteries.

From the New York Criterion. (*Nov.* 10, 1855.)

LEAVES OF GRASS, by Walt Whitman. 1855.

An unconsidered letter of introduction has oftentimes pro-·rured the admittance of a scurvy fellow into good society, and Jur apology for permitting any allusion to the above volume in our columns is, that it has been unworthily recommended by a gentleman of wide repute, and .might, on that account, obtain access to respectable people, unless its real character were exposed.

Mr. Ralph Waldo Emerson either recognizes and accepts these "leaves," as the gratifying result of his own peculiar doctrines, or else he has hastily indorsed them, after a partial and superficial reading. If it is of any importance he may extricate himself from the dilemma. We, however, believe that this book does express the bolder results of a certain transcendental kind of thinking, which some may have styled philosophy.

As to the volume itself, we have only to remark, that it strongly fortifies the doctrines of the Metempsychosists, for it is impossible to imagine how any man's fancy could have conceived such a mass of stupid filth, unless he were possessed of the soul of a sentimental donkey that had died of disappointed love. This *poet* (?) without wit, but with a certain vagrant wildness, just serves to show the energy which natural imbecility is occasionally capable of under strong excitement.

There are too many persons, who imagine they demonstrate their superiority to their fellows, by disregarding all the politenesses and decencies of life, and, therefore, justify themselves in indulging the vilest imaginings and shamefullest license. But Nature, abhorring the abuse of the capacities she has given to man, retaliates upon him, by rendering extravagant indulgence in any direction followed by an insatiable, ever-consuming, and never to be appeased passion.

Thus, to these pitiful beings, virtue and honor are but names. Bloated with self-conceit, they strut abroad unabashed in the daylight, and expose to the world the festering sores that overlay them like a garment. Unless we admit this exhibition to be beautiful, we are at once set down for non-progressive conservatives, destitute of the "inner light," the far-seeingness which, of course, characterizes those gifted individuals. Now, any one who has noticed the tendency of thought in these later years, must be aware that a quantity of this kind of nonsense is being constantly displayed. The immodesty of presumption exhibited by those *seers;* their arrogant pretentiousness; the complacent smile with which they listen to the echo of their own braying, should be, and we believe is, enough to disgust the great majority of sensible folks; but, unfortunately, there is a class that, mistaking sound for sense, attach some importance to all this rant and cant. These candid, these ingenuous, these honest "progressionists;" these human diamonds without flaws; these men that have *come*—detest furiously all shams; "to the pure, all things are pure;" they are pure, and, consequently, must thrust their reeking presence under every man's nose.

They seem to think that man has no instinctive delicacy; is not imbued with a conservative and preservative modesty, that acts as a restraint upon the violence of passions, which for a wise purpose, have been made so strong. No! these fellows have no secrets, no disguises; no, indeed! But they do have, conceal it by whatever language they choose, a degrading, beastly sensuality, that is fast rotting the healthy core of all the social virtues.

There was a time when licentiousness laughed at reproval; now it writes essays and delivers lectures. Once it shunned the light; now it courts attention, writes books showing how grand and pure it is, and prophecies from its lecherous lips its own ultimate triumph.

Shall we argue with such men? Shall we admit them into our houses, that they may leave a foul odor, contaminating the pure, healthful air? Or shall they be placed in the same category with the comparatively innocent slave of poverty, ignorance, and passion that skulks along in the shadows of byways; even in her deep degradation possessing some sparks of the Divine light, the germ of good that reveals itself by a sense of shame?

Thus, then, we leave this gathering of muck to the laws which, certainly, if they fulfil their intent, must have power to suppress such obscenity. As it is entirely destitute of wit, there is nc probability that any would, after this exposure, read it in the hope of finding that; and we trust no one will require further evidence — for, indeed, we do not believe there is a newspaper so vile that would print confirmatory extracts.

In our allusion to this book, we have found it impossible to convey any, even the most faint idea of its style and contents, and of our disgust and detestation of them, without employing language that cannot be pleasing to ears polite; but it does seem that some one should, under circumstances like these, undertake a most disagreeable, yet stern duty. The records of crime show that many monsters have gone on in impunity, because the exposure of their vileness was attended with too great indelicacy. *Peccatum illud horribile, inter Christianos non nominandum.*

From the Cincinnati Commercial. (1860.)

WALT WHITMAN'S POEM.

The author of "Leaves of Grass" has perpetrated another "poem." The N. Y. Saturday Press, in whose columns, we regret to say, it appears, calls it "a curious warble." Curious, it may be ; but warble it is not, in any sense of that mellifluous word. It is a shade less heavy and vulgar than the "Leaves of Grass," whose unmitigated badness seemed to cap the climax of poetic nuisances. But the present performance has all the emptiness, without half the grossness, of the author's former efforts.

How in the name of all the Muses this so-called "poem" ever got into the columns of the Saturday Press, passes our poor comprehension. We had come to look upon that journal as the prince of literary weeklies, the *arbiter elegantiarum* of dramatic and poetic taste, into whose well-filled columns nothing stupid or inferior could intrude. The numerous delicious poems; the sparkling *bon mots;* the puns, juicy and classical, which almost redeemed that vicious practice, and raised it to the rank of a fine art ; the crisp criticisms, and delicate dramatic humors of "Personne," and the charming piquancies of the *spirituelle* Ada Clare — all united to make up a paper of rare excellence. And it is into this gentle garden of the Muses that that unclean cub of the wilderness, Walt Whitman, has been suffered to intrude, trampling with his vulgar and profane hoofs among the delicate flowers which bloom there, and soiling the spotless white of its fair columns with lines of stupid and meaningless twaddle.

Perhaps our readers are blissfully ignorant of the history and achievements of Mr. Walt Whitman. Be it known, then, that he is a native and resident of Brooklyn, Long Island, born and bred in an obscurity from which it were well he never had emerged. A person of coarse nature, and strong, rude passions, he has passed his life in cultivating, not the amenities, but the rudenesses of character ; and instead of tempering his native ferocity with the delicate influences of art and refined literature, he has studied to exaggerate his deformities, and to thrust into his composition all the brute force he could muster from a capacity not naturally sterile in the elements of strength. He has undertaken to be an artist, without learning the first principle of art, and has presumed to put forth "poems," without possessing a spark of the poetic faculty. He affects swagger and independence, and blurts out his vulgar impertinence under a full assurance of "originality."

In his very first performance, this truculent tone was manifested. He exaggerated every sentiment, and piled up with endless repetition every epithet, till the reader grew weary, even to nausea, of his unmeaning rant. He announces himself to the world as a new and striking thinker, who had something to reveal. His "Leaves of Grass" were a revelation from the Kingdom of Nature. Thus he screams to a gaping universe:

"I, Walt Whitman, an American, one of the roughs, a Cosmos; I shout my voice high and clear over the waves; I send my barbaric yawp over the roofs of the world!"

Such was the style of his performance, only it was disfigured by far worse sins of morality than of taste. Never, since the days of Rabelais, was there such literature of uncleanness as some portions of this volume exhibited. All that is beautiful and sacred in love was dragged down to the brutal plane of animal passion, and the writer appeared to revel in language fit only for the lips of the Priapus of the old mythology.

We had hoped that the small reception accorded to his first performance had deterred Mr. Whitman from fresh trespasses in the realms of literature. Several years had passed away; his worse than worthless book had been forgotten, and we hoped that this Apollo of the Brooklyn marshes had returned to his native mud. But we grieve to say he revived last week, and although somewhat changed, changed very little for the better. We do not find so much that is offensive, but we do find a vast amount of irreclaimable drivel and inexplicable nonsense.

We have searched this "poem" through with the serious and deliberate endeavor to find out the reason of its being written ; to discover some clue to the mystery of so vast an expenditure of words. But we honestly confess our utter inability to solve the problem. It is destitute of all the elements which are commonly desiderated in poetical composition ; it has neither rhythm nor melody, rhyme nor reason, metre nor sense. We do solemnly assert, that there is not to be discovered, through- out the whole performance, so much as the glimmering ghost of an idea. Here is the proem, which the author, out of his char- acteristic perversity, insists upon calling the *Pre-verse :*

" Out of the rocked cradle,
Out of the mocking-bird's throat, the musical shuttle,
Out of the boy's mother's womb, and from the nipples of her breasts,
Out of the Ninth-Month midnight,
Over the sterile sea-sands, and the field beyond, where the child, leaving his
    bed, wandered alone, bareheaded, barefoot,
Down from the showered halo and the moonbeams,
Up from the mystic play of shadows twining and twisting as if they were alive,
Out from the patches of briers and blackberries,
From the memories of the bird that chanted to me,
From your memories, sad brother — from the fitful risings and fallings I heard,
From that night, infantile, under the yellow half-moon, late risen, and swollen
    as if with tears,
From those beginning notes of sickness and love, there in the mist,
From the thousand responses in my heart, never to cease,
From the myriad thence-aroused words,
From the word stronger and more delicious than any,
From such, as now they start, the scene revisiting,
As a flock, twittering, rising, or overhead passing,

Borne hither — ere all eludes me, hurriedly,
A man — yet by these tears a little boy again,
Throwing myself on the sand, I,
Confronting the waves, sing."

This is like nothing we ever heard of in literature, unless it be the following lucid and entertaining composition :

"Once there was an old woman went into the garden to get some cabbage to make an apple pie. Just then a great she-bear comes up and pops his head into the shop. 'What, no soap!' So he died, and she married the barber; and there was present at the wedding the Jicaninies and the Piccaninies, and the Grand Panjandrum himself, with the little round button at the top; and they all fell to playing the game of catch as catch can, till the gunpowder ran out of the heels of their boots."

The "poem" goes on, after the same maudlin manner, for a hundred lines or more, in which the interjection "O" is employed about five-and-thirty times, until we reach the following gem :

"Never again leave me to be the peaceful child I was before what there in the
      night,
By the sea, under the yellow and sagging moon,
The dusky demon aroused, the fire, the sweet hell within,
The unknown want, the destiny of me."

O, but this is bitter bad !

            " O give me some clue!
            O if I am to have so much, let me have more!
            O a word! O what is my destination?
            O I fear it is henceforth chaos!"

There is no doubt of it, we do assure you! And, what is more, it never was anything else. Now, what earthly object can there be in writing and printing such unmixed and hopeless drivel as that? If there were any relief to the unmeaning monotony, some glimpse of fine fancy, some oasis of sense, some spark of "the vision and the faculty divine," we would not say a word. But we do protest, in the name of the sanity of the human intellect, against being invited to read such stuff as this, by its publication in the columns of a highly respectable literary journal. What is the comment of the Saturday Press itself on the "poem"? It says :

"Like the 'Leaves of Grass,' the purport of this wild and plaintive song, well enveloped, and eluding definition, is positive and unquestionable, like the effect of music. The piece will bear reading many times — perhaps, indeed, only comes forth, as from recesses, by many repetitions."

Well, Heaven help us, then, for as we are a living man, we would not read that poem "many times" for all the poetry that was ever perpetrated since the morning stars sang together. "Well enveloped, and eluding definition." Indeed! We should think so. For our part, we hope it will remain "well enveloped" till doomsday ; and as for "definition," all we can do in that direction is to declare that either that "poem" is nonsense, or we are a lunatic.

If any of the tuneful Nine have ever descended upon Mr. Walt Whitman, it must have been long before that gentleman reached the present sphere of existence. His amorphous productions clearly belong to that school which it is said that neither gods nor men can endure. There is no meaning discoverable in his writings, and if there were, it would most certainly not be worth the finding out. He is the laureate of the empty deep of the incomprehensible ; over that immortal limbo described by Milton, he has stretched the drag-net of his genius ; and as he has no precedent and no rival, so we venture to hope that he will never have an imitator.

From the Brooklyn City News. (1860.)

A BALLAD OF LONG ISLAND.

Admirers of Walt Whitman's "Leaves of Grass " will find a curious ballad, a new poem, after the same rude and mystical type of versification, in the issue of that literary paper, the New York Saturday Press, for to-day. The piece we allude to, "A Child's Reminiscence," has for its locale, this island of ours, under its old aboriginal name of Paumanok. The plot is a simple one, founded on the advent here, as occasionally happens on "the south side," in the breeding season, of a pair of southern mocking-birds,

> Two guests from Alabama — two together,

Whose nest by the sea-shore, the boy-poet cautiously watches. The gay and wild notes of the he-bird are translated, until his mate disappears. Now the song turns into sadness ; for

> " Thenceforth, all that Spring,
> And all that Summer, in the sound of the sea,
> And at night, under the full of the moon, in calmer weather,
> Over the hoarse surging of the sea,
> Or flitting from brier to brier by day,
> I saw, I heard at intervals, the remaining one, the he-bird,
> The solitary guest from Alabama."

We will not follow the poet's rendering of the bird's warble ; indeed the whole poem needs to be read in its entirety — and several times at that. We will, however, give one detached stanzas, as a specimen of Walt Whitman's versification. It follows the bird's plaintive notes. It brings rapidly and artistically together, in the moonlit midnight, the three leading characters, if we may call them so, of the poem — the Barefoot boy, the Mocking-bird, and the Sea, (the "Savage Old Mother :")

> " The aria sinking,
> All else continuing — the stars shining,
> The winds blowing — the notes of the wondrous bird echoing,
> With angry moans the fierce old mother yet, as ever, incessantly moaning,

On the sands of Paumanok's shore gray and rustling,
The yellow half-moon, enlarged, sagging down, drooping. the face of the sea
　　almost touching,
The boy ecstatic — with his bare feet the waves, with his hair the atmosphere
　　dallying,
The love in the heart pent, now loose, now at last tumultuously bursting,
The aria's meaning, the ears, the soul swiftly depositing,
The strange tears down the cheeks coursing,
The colloquy there — the trio — each uttering,
The undertone — the savage old mother, incessantly crying,
To the boy's soul's questions sullenly timing — some drowned secret hissing,
To the outsetting bard of love."

From the N. Y. Saturday Press. (1860.)

YOURN AND MINE, AND ANY-DAY.

[*A Yawp, after Walt Whitman.*]

1. With antecedents and consequents,
　　With our Fathers, Mothers, Aunts, Uncles, and the family
　　　　at large accumulated by past ages,
　　With all which would have been nothing if anything were
　　　　not something which everything is,
　　With Europe, Asia, Africa, America, Peoria, and New
　　　　Jersey,
　　With the Pre-Adamite, the Yarab, the Guebre, the Hotten-
　　　　tot, the Esquimaux, the Gorilla, and the Nonde-
　　　　scriptian,
　　With antique powwowing, — with laws, jaws, wars, and three-
　　　　tailed bashaws,
　　With the butcher, the baker, the candlestick-maker, and
　　　　Ralph Waldo Carlyle,
　　With the sale of Long Island Railway stock, — with spirit-
　　　　ualists, with the yawper, with the organ-grinder and
　　　　monkey,
　　With everybody and everything in general and nothing and
　　　　nobody in particular, besides otherbodies and things
　　　　too numerous to mention,
　　Yourn and Mine arrived, — The Arrival arrove, and making
　　　　this Nonsense:
　　This Nonsense! sending itself ahead of any sane compre-
　　　　hension this side of Jordan.

2. O, but it is not the Nonsense — it is Mine, — it is Yourn,
　　We touch all "effects," and tally all bread-sticks,
　　We are the Etceteras and Soforths, — we easily include them,
　　　　and more;
　　All obfusticates around us, — there is as much as possible of
　　　　a muchness;
　　The entire system of the universe discomboborates around
　　　　us with a perfect looseness.

As for Mine,
Mine has the idea of my own, and what's Mine is my own,
    and my own is all Mine and believes in it all,
Mine believes meum is true, and rejects nix.

4. Has Mine forgotten to grab any part?
Fork over then whoever and whatever is worth having, till
    Mine gives a receipt in full.

5. Mine respects Brahma, Vishnu, Mumbo-Jumbo, and the great
    Panjandrum,
Mine adopts things generally which are claimed by Yourn,
Mine asserts that these should have been my own in all past
    days,
And that they could not no how have been nobody else's,
And that to-day is neither yesterday nor to-morrow, — and
    that I-S is is.

6. In the name of Dogberry, — and in Mine and Yourn, — Bosh!
And in the name of Bombastes Furioso, — and in Yourn
    and Mine, — Gas!

7. Mine knows that Dogberry was an Ass, and Bombastes Fu-
    rioso a likewise,
And that both curiously conjoint in the present time, in
    Yourn and Mine,
And that where Mine is, or Yourn is, this present day, there
    is the centre of all Asininities,
And there is the meaning to us, of all that has ever come of
    Yourn and Mine, or ever will come.

                      -SAERASMID, *Philadelphia.*

From " Waifs from Washington."— by UMOS.

WALT WHITMAN'S YAWP. The review by the Cincinnati
Commercial of Walt Whitman's last yawp, which (the review)
you were frank enough to print in your last issue, emboldens
me to speak my sentiments. When I opened the Press containing that extraordinary concentration of words, I said to
myself, here's something nice for Mrs. U. to listen to, this night,
after the little U.'s have curled themselves up in bed. Accordingly, the desired hour having arrived, I opened the Press, and
inquired of Mrs. U. what she knew of Walt Whitman, and I
am happy to say, — happy, after reading what the Cincinnati
paper says about his " Leaves of Grass," — that she instantly
disclaimed the remotest acquaintance with any one of that
name. " Then," I proceeded to remark, " he must be a poetic

luminary of the first magnitude — a sort of Fresnel light — who has been, like Alexander Smith, hiding his brilliancy under dry-goods boxes or flour-barrels, and now blazes forth to amaze the readers of the Saturday Press, and the rest of mankind. Listen; it's good, or it wouldn't be here."

I began. . . .

Last Winter I got on skates, my first appearance before an icy audience for fifteen years.

Happily for me, I selected the night and a retired spot. Unhappily, that the — infernal, I was going to say, hyperborean is better — hyperborean idea ever entered my wretched head; and for its weakness that head paid a fearful penalty.

I cherish a vivid remembrance, that on that fearful night there was an *irrepressible conflict* between my several members. No two of them would go the same way, and when they did, it was not the way I wanted them to go. The only consentaneous movement which they seemed at all disposed to execute, was a spasmodic, unsolicited, and uncontrollable flight *ad astra*, in which my head foolishly refused to participate, and for its contumacy was left behind, the stars being so obliging as to come down in dazzling throngs to gaze upon my helplessness. I remembered the story of Miller at Lundy's Lane, of Bruce (was it?) and the historical Spider, who tried twenty times before he hauled himself up, and I didn't give it up so, O Editor! but "tried, tried again," until I believe the closed-up sutures in my cranium were opened as widely as if the brains were out, and a pint of white beans were in, with the whole, *caput-al*, arrangement soaking in the anatomist's basin. Such a wild, heterogeneous, insane, Saint Vitus-like, *poly*-maniacal orgie, as my shapely and generally well-behaved branches went into that night, will never be forgotten.

I said I began to read Walt Whitman's Yawp.

Pardon my digression — I have been trying to say that I felt as I was reading, that Walt — whatever that stands for — was on his *musical* skates for the first time.

O Shakespeare, O Milton, O Longfellow, O Henry Clapp, Jr., Editor of the nicest paper in the country, — I couldn't see it!

I told Mrs. U. so — I asked her what you, O Editor, meant by publishing such wretched trumpery? She had not been favored with your confidence, and said she didn't know. But she didn't think it trumpery — she thought there was something in it.

As Mrs. U. is the poet of my concern, her suggestion to that effect was a strong point in favor of Mr. Whitman's barbaric Yawp.

So I attempted the Yawp again.

Like as Mr. Webster, said to the dandy who asked him if he never danced, "I never had intellect enough to learn," so I say

— and I say it with grateful humility — "I haven't poetry enough to understand Walt's Yawp. More than that, I don't want to."

From the New York Tribune. (1859.)

The Boston Courier thinks it very likely that the poet Walt Whitman, as is reported, now drives a Broadway omnibus, and says:

"Whitman's extraordinary abilities have always been fettered by an unconquerable laziness. The last time we saw him he was mounted upon a Brooklyn omnibus, his legs hanging over the side, and his body resting comfortably upon his elbow. He appeared to be absorbed in an ecstatic contemplation of his own greatness. His dress was wonderful beyond description; high heavy boots, tight trousers, an unprecedented rough jacket, and a tapering tower of a hat. It was said last winter that he was getting up a series of lectures, but it seems that his natural indolence has conquered his poetic inspirations."

From the New York Constellation. (1859.)

AN OMNIBUS DRIVER OR NOT? — A leading journal in this city has recently been duped by a communication, or a statement manufactured in its own office, into saying that Walt Whitman, the writer of "Leaves of Grass," one of the most remarkable and original contributions to our literature for many years, was driving an omnibus.

Now, whether he has ever done so or not, we neither know nor care; but certain are we that he is not, at present, doing so, as we have ourselves repeatedly seen and conversed with him in the course of the present month. Moreover, we will put the question frankly forward, whether, if he chose to earn his bread and salt by so doing, it ought, necessarily, to be commented upon by the daily press. If we chose to occupy the position of a barber, or keep a lager beer saloon, should such a mode of gaining our living be cited to our discredit. In Europe it has never been so cited. (Mark Lemon was an alehouse-keeper; Ferguson, a shepherd; Crawshay, an errand-boy; Burns, a ploughman; Thiers and Guizot, newspaper editors, &c., &c.) And we regard the attempt to stain the supposititious act with a ludicrous celebrity, as having been made in the very worst of tastes.

www.ingramcontent.com/pod-product-compliance
Lightning Source LLC
Chambersburg PA
CBHW032045090426
42733CB00030B/708